Jonathan Swift

Revised Edition

Twayne's English Authors Series

Bertram H. Davis, Editor
Florida State University

TEAS 42

JONATHAN SWIFT
1667–1745
Courtesy of the National Portrait Gallery

Jonathan Swift

Revised Edition

By Robert Hunting

University of Maine

Twayne Publishers
A Division of G. K. Hall & Co. • *Boston*

Jonathan Swift, Revised Edition
Robert Hunting

Copyright 1989 by G. K. Hall & Co.
All rights reserved.
Published by Twayne Publishers
A Division of G. K. Hall & Co.
70 Lincoln Street
Boston, Massachusetts 02111

Copyediting supervised by Barbara Sutton
Book production by Gabrielle B. McDonald
Book design by Barbara Anderson

Typeset in 11 pt. Garamond
by Huron Valley Graphics, Ann Arbor, Michigan

Library of Congress Cataloging-in-Publication Data

Hunting, Robert.
    Jonathan Swift / by Robert Hunting.—Rev. ed.
        p.   cm.—(Twayne's English authors series ; TEAS 42)
    Bibliography: p.
    Includes index.
    ISBN 0-8057-6982-X (alk. paper)
    1. Swift, Jonathan, 1667–1745—Criticism and interpretation.
    I. Title. II. Series.
    PR3727.H8   1989
    828'.509—dc20   89-2126
                                                                      CIP

For C. S. and M.

Contents

About the Author

Robert Hunting received his Ph.D. from Brown University in 1951, has taught at Duke and Purdue universities, and served as chair of the English Department at the University of Maine. In upper-level courses and seminars he taught major eighteenth-century figures like Swift, Pope, Johnson, Sterne, and Austen; he has also contributed a wide scattering of reviews, notes, and articles to such publications as the *Philological Quarterly, Notes and Queries, Boston University Studies in English, Modern Language Notes, English Literature in Transition, Western Humanities Review, Criticism,* and *Études anglaises.*

Professor Hunting's numerous pedagogical articles have appeared in *College English,* the *English Journal, College Composition and Communication,* and elsewhere. He has edited two books: an edition of *Boswell's "Life of Johnson"* (1969) and *Dorando, A Spanish Tale* (1974). Hunting is now professor emeritus at the University of Maine. Like Sir William Temple, Jonathan Swift's patron, he is also a beekeeper.

Preface

In assembling the materials for the first edition of this book I relied very heavily on an impressive body of historical criticism, but my approach was only incidentally that of the historical critic. My aim in the first place was, rather, to view in a loosely chronological order the eternally contemporaneous of Swift's writings—those works that speak most interestingly and often very insistently to our times. My aim in the second place was to indicate as little as possible the right and the wrong way to read these works and, as much as possible, what might be termed an area of interpretation, in and for our time, that a thoughtful reading invites.

These criteria obligated me to avoid—or, at least, to touch only lightly upon—a large number of often quite alluring historical, bibliographical, and biographical questions and a number of writings (like *The Conduct of the Allies*) that reward study but are so closely tied to their times that they were outside the scope of my original study. (However, one convenient but unplanned result of these limitations was that the study of the writings upon which I had focused could be regarded as just about a semester's work in a course on Swift.) The plan of the book also forced me to make no more than passing comment on the many literary influences at work on Swift and about Swift's influence on literary figures who followed him.

In the more than two decades since the first edition of *Jonathan Swift* appeared, many of my opinions about Swift and his works have changed. Numerous new and distinguished articles and books on Swift have become available. Irvin Ehrenpreis completed his monumental three-volume *Swift: The Man, His Works, The Age,* and valuable one-volume commentaries such as those by J. A. Downie (*Jonathan Swift: Political Writer*) and David Nokes (*Jonathan Swift, a Hypocrite Reversed*) have been published. Resources for the study of Swift's considerable output of poetry have also been richly increased by the appearance of a large number of excellent articles and books.

This edition has been very substantially revised and reflects my opinions as they have changed over the years; it also reports on and—insofar as competence and space permit—reflects the abundant new scholarship and criticism now available. The commentary, throughout, has been somewhat—though I hope not unnecessarily—extended.

My way of approaching Swift's works is essentially unchanged from what it always has been. Despite an attraction to this or that critical stance, I seem always to come back to the position taken by my favorite professor, the late Austin Warren. In the preface to his *Connections* (1970) he wrote, "As a literary critic, I have no 'method,' no specialty, but [am] what is called, in another discipline, a 'general practitioner.' Literary theory and methodology have ever interested me; but, confronted with the situation of 'practical criticism,' I look through my repertory for the methods and the mixture of methods appropriate to the case before me . . . ." If many of us do not have Austin Warren's astonishing "repertory," we can nonetheless appreciate his sane, tolerant, and eclectic position. It is my position in this book.

My hope is that readers will say that the seven chapters between these covers are, to use a circumlocution of one my favorite friends, "not entirely without merit." If the circumlocution is at all applicable, then this book may encourage an interest in both Swift the man and Swift the writer. That would be good, for then some readers will go on to enjoy better and in all senses bigger books than mine could ever be about this most interesting, disturbing, and perplexing of the Augustans.

Every writer must envy the assurance with which Montaigne was able to deceive himself in his *Essays:* "Reader, this is an honest book." I have tried to make my book honest; I hope it is. At least in matters where honesty is relatively easy, I should most especially like not to err. Therefore, wherever in the following pages an interpretation of a fact or of a pattern of facts is my own, I have tried to indicate this as diffidently as possible. Also in the very many places where I have referred to useful discoveries or insights of the great Swift scholars and critics of our and earlier times, I have tried always to indicate that indebtedness. My obligation to these men and women is enormous; for in common with all Swift students, I have perforce relied heavily on the absolutely indispensable contributions to Swift studies made by such people as Émile Pons, F. Elrington Ball, Harold Williams, Ricardo Quintana, Herbert Davis, Kathleen Williams, Louis Landa, Maurice Johnson, Irvin Ehrenpreis, and many others. I am also indebted, though in different ways, to the ideas received over the years from my students; to the thoughtful, patient, and meticulous editors who have worked with me on this book (I think particularly of Professor Bertram H. Davis); and to Constance Coulter Hunting.

Robert Hunting

University of Maine

Chronology

1680–1740	Approximate terminal dates of the English Augustan Age. F. R. Leavis writes of this age, "A metropolitan fashionable Society, compact and politically in the ascendant, found itself in charge of standards, and extremely convinced that, in the things it cared about, there were standards to be observed, models to be followed: it was anxious to be civilized on the best models" (*Revaluations,* 112–13). Chief literary figures: Dryden, Congreve, Addison, Steele, Gay, Defoe, Pope, and of course Swift.
1667	Jonathan Swift born in Dublin Ireland, 30 November, to Abigaile and, posthumously, Jonathan Swift.
1673(?)–1681	Attends Kilkenny Grammar School.
1679	Whig and Tory parties originate.
1682–1686	Swift attends Trinity College, Dublin.
1688	The Glorious Revolution; the reign of William and Mary (1688–1702) begins.
1689	Becomes secretary in the house of Sir William Temple, Moor Park, Surrey, England. Here he probably first meets Esther Johnson ("Stella"), whom he tutors during the years with Temple.
1690	Returns to Ireland on the advice of his doctors.
1691	Back in England; returns to Moor Park.
1692	Receives M.A. from Oxford. First known published poem, "Ode to the Athenian Society."
1695	Ordained priest in the Church of Ireland (the Irish branch of the Anglican Church). Becomes vicar of Kilroot in northern Ireland. Involved with Jane Waring.
1696	Returns to Moor Park; probably composes most of *A Tale of a Tub.*
1698	Resigns the living at Kilroot.

1699	Temple dies. Swift returns to Ireland.
1700	Installed as vicar at Laracor and rceives the prebend of Dunlavin in St. Patrick's Cathedral, Dublin.
1701	Esther Johnson and Rebecca Dingley settle in Dublin.
1702	Awarded D.D. from Dublin University.
1702–1714	Reign of Queen Anne.
1704	Battle of Blenheim—a great victory for Marlborough and the English. *A Tale of a Tub* and *The Battle of the Books* published anonymously.
1707	In London, as emissary of the Irish clergy, seeks remission of the First Fruits. Meets Esther Vanhomrigh (?).
1708	*The Partridge-Bickerstaff Papers. An Argument against Abolishing Christianity.*
1709	Back at Laracor. "A Description of the Morning."
1710	Tories come to power. Swift returns to England. Renounces Whigs and joins the Tories. Edits the *Examiner,* the Tory newspaper. Begins *The Journey to Stella* (continued from 1 September 1710 to 6 June 1713).
1710	"A Description of a City Shower."
1711	*The Conduct of the Allies; Miscellanies in Prose and Verse; A New Journey to Paris.* Continues visits at Vanhomrigh home.
1712	"Cadenus and Vanessa" begun (?) (published 1727).
1713	Treaty of Utrecht ends the War of the Spanish Succession. A disappointed Swift is appointed Dean of St. Patrick's Cathedral, Dublin.
1714	Scriblerus Club formed. Swift returns to Ireland, followed soon after by Esther Vanhomrigh. Reign of George I begins (1714–27). Long Whig supremacy under Walpole begins.
1716	Presumed by some biographers to have married Stella.
1720	*A Proposal for the Universal Use of Irish Manufacture;* probably begins writing *Gulliver's Travels.*
1721	*A Letter to a Young Gentleman, Lately Entered into Holy Orders.*

1722	"Satirical Elegy on the Death of a Late Famous General."
1723	*A Letter to a Young Lady on Her Marriage.* Esther Vanhomrigh dies.
1724–1725	Publishes *The Drapier Letters;* Wood's halfpence defeated.
1726	Visits England, where he is Alexander Pope's houseguest. *Gulliver's Travels* published.
1727	Last trip to England. *Miscellanies,* vols. 1 and 2, published ("Cadenus and Vanessa" included in this publication). Reign of George II begins (1727–60).
1728	Esther Johnson dies.
1729	"A Pastoral Dialogue"; *A Modest Proposal.*
1731	"Verses on the Death of Dr. Swift." Writes a number of other poems, including such scatological productions as "A Beautiful Young Nymph Going to Bed" and "Strephon and Chloe."
1732	"A Lady's Dressing Room."
1735	Collected edition of Swift's *Works* published in Dublin by George Faulkner.
1736	"A Character, Panegyric, and Description of the Legion Club."
1738	*A Compleat Collection of Genteel and Ingenious Conversation.* Swift's mental powers are failing.
1742	Guardians in Chancery appointed to care for Swift's affairs.
1745	Dies, 19 October.

Chapter One
Life and Literature for Our Times

By responding to a challenge in 1708, Jonathan Swift made an immortal footnote out of an outrageous scamp whose name would otherwise have been by now long forgotten. The footnote in question concerns a cobbler who had become a highly successful maker of almanacs and had challenged his readers three times—in 1699, in 1704, and in 1706—to compete with him at prophecy. In 1708 Swift took up the challenge, not only I suppose for the fun he could have in attacking an arrant hypocrite, and not only because he very commonly felt a compulsion to unmask fakery, but also because Partridge had attacked the Church of England and its clergy—and Swift was a clergyman, and the Church of England was his church.

The hilarious unmasking of John Partridge is an instructive introduction to characteristic Swiftean procedures and attitudes. First, in the invented role of Isaac Bickerstaff, Swift prophesied the death of Partridge. It was, he wrote, "but a trifle; yet I will mention it. . . . [Partridge] will infallibly die upon the 29th of March next, about eleven at Night, of a raging fever."[1] In his next move he adopted another pose and reported "the accomplishment of the first of Mr. Bickerstaff's predictions": Partridge was dead. "Mr. Bickerstaff was mistaken almost four Hours in his Calculation. In other Circumstances he was exact enough."[2] Swift did not, even at this point, let up; he also celebrated his victim's "death" with an elegy:

> Here Five Foot deep lyes on his Back
> A Cobler, Starmonger, and Quack,
> Who to the Stars in pure Good-will,
> Does to his best look upward still.
> Weep all you customers that use
> His pills, his almanacks or shoes.
> (1708)

So convincing was this merciless hazing that the Stationer's Register, which listed names of those authorized to print something for sale, apparently removed Partridge's name from their rolls. Poor Partridge himself, however, remained quite stubbornly unconvinced and in his 1709 almanac vigorously protested that he was alive; but Swift would have none of this. In *A Vindication of Isaac Bickerstaff, Esq.*, he conclusively proved the man's death and ridiculed Partridge for not having the sense to admit it: "He is the *only* person," wrote the satirist, "from whom I have heard . . . Objection. . . ."[3]

Jonathan Swift, the perpetrator of this weird and hugely successful hoax, was to spend a large part of his life defending his church from attackers. All his long life he invented and put on masks—as Bickerstaff, Gulliver, the Drapier—that fooled nobody for long; but through them he effectively made known his ideas and attitudes. All his life he attacked pretense and pleaded with people to see that "It is not as you think—look!"[4] His hope was that, if people looked, they would see behind the successful almanac-maker, the charlatan; beneath the rind, the kernel; behind the appearance, the reality. That Swift sometimes ignored or even perverted his own teaching does not detract from his preachment. No one, ever, has said more powerfully what this man had to say.

Swift's Background

Jonathan Swift was born on 30 November 1667, in Hoey's Alley, in Dublin, Ireland. Born after the death of his father, he was the second child and first son of English parents who had moved to Ireland. Thus far most, if not all, biographers agree. Almost immediately, however, fiction has often taken over. A great number of fictional lives of Swift have, in fact, been written. The point may be illustrated by reference to one of the most fanciful of them. It is by Elbert Hubbard (1856–1915) who, in his *Little Journeys to the Homes of the Great*, wrote,

His father married at twenty. His income matched his years—it was just twenty pounds per annum. His wife was a young girl, bright, animated, intelligent.

In a few short months this girl carried in her arms a baby [Jane, Swift's sister]. This baby was wrapped in a tattered shawl and cried piteously from hunger, for the mother had not enough to eat. She was cold, and sick, and in disgrace. Her husband, too, was ill, and sorely in debt. It was midwinter.

When Spring came, and the flowers blossomed, and the birds mated, and warm breezes came whispering softly from the South, and all the earth was glad, the husband of this child-wife was in his grave, and she was alone. Alone? No; she carried in her arms the hungry babe, and beneath her heart she felt the faint flutter of another life.[5]

That "faint flutter" was Jonathan Swift.

An altogether different sort of account may be found in Phyllis Greenacre's *Swift and Carroll, a Psychoanalytic Study of Two Lives.* Among other interesting theses, Dr. Greenacre suggests that "Swift apparently suffered from severe anxiety and diffuse hypochondriasis of the type which so often accompanies an unusually severe castration complex, in which pregenital determinants are strong."[6] Dr. Greenacre also says that "Swift's early life would certainly predispose to the development of a stunting bisexuality, as indeed his mature years showed. That there was further fixation at the anal level and an extreme impairment of genital functioning is indicated in his character and his writings."[7] Such comments are difficult to prove, and particularly so in this instance because of insufficient and even inexact use of supporting evidence. For example, the use of the *Memoirs of Scriblerus* as evidence is most distressing since there were six other writers involved in the composition of that book; moreover, authorship of the various contributions has never been entirely settled. But even though I have some doubts about Greenacre's conclusions, I think I should note them carefully. If they do not explain matters to my satisfaction, they do at least highlight problems for which I confess I do not have better explanations. There is no doubt that Swift had serious and lifelong problems of a psychiatric sort, as evidenced by his frequent and very insistent reminders of the animality we all share, by the "excremental vision" that informs much of his work, and by his ambiguous attitude toward women. Our psychoanalytical critics and biographers may yet be of help, but, as my remarks here and there in this text will show, my inclination thus far is to view their comments with a mix of interest, hope, amusement, and skepticism.

Reared in Dublin by his relatives, Swift attended Kilkenny Grammar School and, later, Trinity College, Dublin. He could not have received, in Ireland, a better education; but he appears to have been no more than a run-of-the-mill student. At Trinity College he insulted a junior dean and was obliged publicly, on bended knee, to beg the dean's pardon.[8] Although he did well in languages and literature, he did poorly in what he disliked: abstract philosophy and formal rhetoric.[9] In February 1686 he did receive his degree, though "by special grace," as every biographer points out; yet "this favour," Irvin Ehrenpreis shows, "was by no means uncommon." In Swift's class of thirty-eight students, five graduated "*speciali gratia.*"[10] Thus Swift was himself misleading in the fragment of an autobiography he prepared in 1714: "When the time came for taking his degree of Batchlor . . . he was stopped of his Degree, for Dullness and Insufficiency, and at last hardly admitted in a manner little to his Credit, which is called in that College *Specialia gratia*. . . ."[11]

During most of the decade ending in 1699, Swift was secretary to a retired statesman, Sir William Temple, at Moor Park, Surrey, in England. Temple (1628–99) was one of the great statesmen of the seventeenth century and is remembered for his work in organizing the triple alliance (England, Holland, Sweden) and for arranging the marriage of William of Orange and Mary. Esther Johnson ("Stella") and, later, Swift were inhabitants of his home during his years of retirement at Moor Park. On his behalf, as we shall see, Swift engaged himself in the "war" between the ancients and the moderns in *The Battle of the Books*. After Temple's death, he edited his patron's *Letters* (1701). His long stay with this great man was interrupted several times, most notably from May 1694 to May 1696, during which time he was in Ireland. There he confirmed his decision to seek a career in the Anglican Church of Ireland and in time preferment, he no doubt hoped, to a deanery or even to a bishopric in England. In Dublin on 13 January 1695 he was ordained priest and on 28 January, two weeks later, he was presented to the Prebend of Kilroot. He was installed into his benefice on 15 March 1695.

The assignment to Kilroot—in northern Ireland, near Belfast—turned out to be a disappointment, but nonetheless for two reasons it was important. First, his probably already strong dislike for religious dissenters seems to have been intensified exponentially by his experience in his miserable little parish (the Kilroot church was in ruins!) with tiny congregations that were, like him, part of a minority group in an area dense with Presbyterians whom Swift as usual dismissed contemptuously, as he did all dissidents, as intolerant fanatics. Second, during his brief tenure at Kilroot Swift became engaged to Jane Waring, the first in a line of frail and fatherless young ladies with whom he was to establish a characteristically equivocal relationship. In April 1696 he proposed marriage to Jane Waring, whom he called

"Varina," for it was to be his way to give pet names to his frail and fatherless young ladies. He was perhaps encouraged to think of marriage less because of Varina's charms and more because of the example set by his cousin Thomas Swift, whose recent ordination had been followed by his marriage. As David Nokes says, "if Swift was to consolidate his new choice of life, then marriage was an obvious next step."[12]

The best source of information about the Swift–Varina relationship is epistolary: on record are two letters he wrote to her. This evidence is certainly not very considerable, but it is more than enough to indicate that Varina was a wise twenty-one-year-old when she recognized increasingly serious reservations about her increasingly reluctant suitor, nearly a third older than she. The letters make curious reading. In the first (29 April 1696) he tells his loved one that he has a chance to return to his service with Sir William Temple, so marriage must occur immediately: "if I leave this Kingdom before you are mine, I will endure the utmost indignities of fortune rather than ever return again. . . ."[13] In the second (4 May 1700) he decreed a set of stipulations: "Are you in a condition to manage domestic affairs, with an income of less (perhaps) than three hundred pounds a year? Have you such an inclination to my person and Humour, as to comply with my desires and way of living? Will you be ready to engage in those methods I shall direct for the improvement of your mind?"[14] Finally, if Jane Waring can answer all the questions affirmatively, then, her suitor tells her, "I shall be blessed to have you in my arms, without regarding whether your person be beautiful, or your fortune large."[15] Miss Waring's response is not on record. In any case, the affair (such as it was) ended. Swift remained at Moor Park.

The years with Temple were significant in that turbulent age not only because of the urbane and civilizing influence of the Temple household, but also because they were years when Swift could (and did) read widely in the Temple library; because he had opportunity to find what he was, and was not, as a poet; because he discovered his gifts as a satirist—most of a *A Tale of a Tub* was written during these years (though not published until 1704); and because he there met Esther Johnson. Though conclusive evidence is lacking, he is presumed by many biographers to have married Esther Johnson ("Stella" was Swift's pet name for her) in 1716.

Shortly after Temple's death (1699) Esther Johnson and her friend Rebecca Dingley (she was older than Stella) had settled permanently in Dublin, near Swift. Harold Williams states that Swift and Stella "observed an almost exaggerated propriety. Whether at Dublin or Laracor [a living that was presented to Swift in 1700], the ladies were free of his lodgings, or house, only when Swift was away. In Dublin, upon his return, they removed elsewhere; or, when he was in the country, they found rooms in nearby Trim, occupied a little cottage at Laracor, or were the guests of Dr. Raymond. Further, Swift hardly allowed himself at any time to be left alone in the same room with Stella."[16] In these almost unbelievable terms, the relationship continued for more than a quarter of a century. The facts of the relationship, as far as we know them, so cry out for interpretation and resolution that it is no wonder that so much has been written on the subject. I have no new evidence to offer and therefore must leave the problem unresolved. However, it will be impossible not to comment further on this matter in discussions, in chapters that follow, on *The Journal to Stella* and on the quite moving poems that Swift addressed to her.

During the Moor Park years Swift also experienced the first of those terrible attacks that—as with Dostoyevski and his epilepsy or Chekhov and his tuberculosis—were to afflict him all his mature years. Swift describes his illness thus in his autobiographical fragment: "For he [Swift] happened before twenty years old, by a Surfeit of fruit to contract a giddyness and coldness of Stomach, that almost brought him to his Grave, and this disorder pursued him with Intermissions of two or three years to the end of his Life."[17] The "Surfeit of fruit" is unlikely to have been the cause of a lifelong misery. Opinion is now general that the suffering was caused by Ménière's disease, a disturbance of the inner ear, the symptoms of which are giddiness and vertigo. The disease had then, and has now, no known cure. However, people who suffer from it are told today to take the pills that are more commonly prescribed against seasickness. "And then," Ehrenpreis reports, "they usually have no trouble."[18] In an era that knew nothing of this simple palliative, Swift suffered his "trouble" through all his adult life.

1708–1714

The years 1708 to 1714 were among the most exciting in Swift's lengthy career. He was in London much of this time, having been sent there as a petitioner for the Church of Ireland. As petitioner his charge was to achieve if possible a remission of what were called the First Fruits and Twentieth Parts. He was to seek, in short, a cancellation of a tax due from every person when first appointed to an ecclesiastical benefice. This was a fixed tax in Swift's time, though earlier it had amounted to a twentieth part of the annual income of a benefice. The tax was paid directly to the Crown of England and it drained the Irish clergy of, Swift estimated, one thousand pounds annually.[19]

In his attempts to get this tax remitted Swift became involved with the Whigs and then, since he was a man of innately conservative bent, with the Tories. (Also, the Tories were willing to grant his petition, though for years it rankled with Swift that he got no credit for his considerable part in that achievement.) These were, in addition, the years of *The Bickerstaff Papers;* of the beginnings of a long and tortuous involvement with a young lady named Esther Vanhomrigh ("Vanessa" was Swift's pet name for her and the name he used in his uneasy poem "Cadenus and Vanessa") of two fine poems, "A Description of the Morning" and "A Description of a City Shower"; of the editorship of the Tory journal the *Examiner;* of that brilliant piece of Tory pamphleteering *The Conduct of the Allies;* of *The Journal to Stella;* and so on. These were exciting days of close association with the chief ministers of England: Robert Harley, Earl of Oxford and Henry St. John, Viscount Bolingbroke. As Swift wrote in his *Four Last Years,* "It was my lot to have been daily conversant with the persons then in power; never absent in times of business or conversation, until a few weeks before her Majesty's death; and a witness of almost every step they made in the course of their administration. . . ."[20] Therefore, when he writes about princes, about politics, about government—as he does in *A Tale of a Tub,* in *Gulliver's Travels,* and in many of his poems and essays—he does so with the authority gained by considerable experience. There is no doubt that the ministry regarded him as an important and an influential figure, but he exaggerates when he claims to be a "witness of almost every step" taken by the chief ministers. For example, though he wrote that Harley and Bolingbroke had no correspondence with the Pretender to the throne of England, the fact is that they were both guilty of treasonable communications with him. The chief ministers simply chose not to tell everything to the Irish vicar of Laracor.[21]

These were also the days of close and happy friendship with some of the greatest wits and writers of the day. With a half dozen or so of these talented men—Parnell, Pope, Prior, Arbuthnot, and Gay, perhaps joined on occasion by Harley (Lord Oxford) and Bishop Atterbury—Swift in 1714 formed the famous Scriblerus Club, "where," as Ehrenpreis says, "the excitement of getting to know people with complex and interesting minds was a pleasure felt by them all."[22] The purpose of the

club could not have been merely convivial, for, as Pope later revealed to
Spence, it also undertook to produce the "Memoirs of Martinus
Scriblerus," wherein would be ridiculed "all the false tastes in learning,
under the character of a man of capacity enough, that had dipped into
every art and science, but injudiciously in each."[23] Consistent with this
intention were references to the possibility of a burlesque of an imagi-
nary voyage, a very distant hint of what Swift was to accomplish a
decade later with his *Gulliver's Travels*.

These were years, finally, of professional disappointment. In a generation when a worldly church lived contentedly with the concept that
churchly offices were political spoils,[24] Swift, who had so brilliantly
served his party, had good reason to expect the reward of a deanery or a
bishopric in England. Instead, in 1713, he was given a deanery in
Dublin. For this failure, Swift himself blamed the Duchess of Somerset
and John Sharp, Archbishop of York, who, he believed, had called
Queen Anne's attention unfavorably to *A Tale of a Tub*. Other factors
were no doubt involved. At any rate, it was back to Ireland that Swift
went, in 1714, to "die," as he later reported, "like a poisoned rat in a
hole."[25] He was forty-seven years old. To Stella he wrote, ". . . neither
can I feel Joy at passing my days in [Ireland], . . . and I confess I
thought the Ministry would not let me go; but perhaps th[e]y cant help
it."[26]

Of course they could have helped it, and probably would have, if Swift
had played his cards more prudently. He should not have brutally insulted the Duchess of Somerset, who was known to be a close friend to the
Queen; in *A Tale of a Tub* he should not have allowed himself to appear an
enemy of his, and his Queen's, church. When Lord Somers wanted an
honest opinion from Swift, Swift gave it, but he would have been better
served had he not done so, for he knew that his Lordship would disagree
and had the power to prevent his rise in the church.[27] Such actions hurt
him. Though he was inordinately sure of his talents and considered them
deserving of reward, and though he ached for recognition and did indeed
get it, the recognition was—paradoxically—never companioned by the
preferment he so ardently desired.

1714–1745

The thirty-one years from 1714 to 1745 were the Irish years that
began, as has been noted, with a period of some considerable hurt and
disappointment. However, always the conscientious clergyman, Swift

busied himself with deanery chores. And, though during the first few years he wrote little, he did as usual exercise regularly, even when the weather was bad: there were always the deanery stairs where he could walk up and down, up and down, and up and down again.[28] Personal cleanliness being important to him, he no doubt continued to wash himself "with," as Samuel Johnson caustically wrote in his *Life of Swift,* "oriental scrupulosity." His circle of friends was gradually enlarged and included such people as Archbishop William King, Charles Ford, Daniel Jackson, Knightley Chetwode, Patrick Delany, Thomas Sheridan, the Rochfort and Grattan families, in addition to Stella and Rebecca Dingley. Enigmatically on the edge of things, but always very much present for yet nearly a decade, was also Esther Vanhomrigh, the unhappy "Vanessa," who fell in love with Swift during his London years and who followed him to Ireland soon after he became dean.

In the poem "To Charles Ford Esq. on His Birth-day" (1723) Swift wrote,

> I thought my very Spleen would burst
> When fortune hither [to Ireland] drove me first;
> Was full as hard to please as You,
> Nor Persons Names, nor Places knew;
> but now I act as other Folk,
> Like Pris'ners when their Gall is broke.

The words reveal that Swift had slowly reconciled himself to his life in Ireland. Indeed, life was far from over for him. The 1720s ushered in a period of almost unbelievable creativity that resulted in the writing of *Gulliver's Travels* (published 1726); much of his best poetry, including "A Beautiful Young Nymph Going to Bed" (1721), "Satirical Elegy on the Death of a Late Famous General" (1722), and "On Poetry: A Rapsody" (1733); and works on behalf of the Irish. Sadness, however, was inevitable. Vanessa's presence plagued him until her death in 1723, and his dearest friend, the lovely Stella, died in 1727.

Swift, the great "Irish Patriot," occasionally gives the impression that Irish affairs did not interest him. In 1714 he had written to Ford, saying, "I hope I shall keep my Resolution of never medling with Irish Politics."[29] But in 1719 to the same good friend he wrote, "No cloyster is retired enough to keep politics out."[30] Obviously the dean's opinion had changed, and of course his own very considerable activities in behalf of the Irish support this impression. Breaking his long silence after the retreat from England in 1714 was his *Proposal for the Universal Use of Irish Manufacture* (1720), and in 1724–25 came *The Drapier Letters*, whereby he successfully contributed to the organization of Irish resistance to the importation of a new copper coin, which would enormously profit one William Wood but leave Ireland with, Swift believed, a debased and inflated currency. The patent for the importation was withdrawn and all of Ireland cheered Swift, who had now become an Irish hero. A little later, in 1729, were published both his *A Proposal That All the Ladies and Women of Ireland Should Appear Constantly in Irish Manufactures* and *A Modest Proposal*. In addition, his poetry and correspondence confirm his often irritated but abiding fascination with Irish affairs.

However, one is tempted to make of this "Hibernian patriot" a different kind of patriot than he really was. Swift was no fiery revolutionary. In his *Of Publick Absurdityes* in England he wrote:

I am grossly deceived if any sober man of very moderate talents, when he reflects upon the many ridiculous hurtfull maxims, customs, and generall rules of life which prevail in this kingdom, would not with great reason be tempted, according to the present turn of his humor, either to laugh, lament, or be angry, or if he were sanguin enough, perhaps to dream of a remedy. It is the mistake of wise and good men that they expect some Reason and Virtue from human nature, than taking it in the bulk, it is in any sort capable of.[31]

The attitude reflected in this characteristically pessimistic and conservative comment is perhaps the sort of thing that impelled George Orwell to make his revealing remark: "[Swift's] implied aim [in his writings] is a static, incurious civilization—the world of his own day, a little cleaner, a little saner, with no radical change and no poking into the unknowable."[32]

When Swift speaks on behalf of the Irish, we should not expect to hear notes quite out of his range. In fairness we should be more reasonable in our expectations than was Orwell, for what Orwell wanted to hear were notes out of most people's range in those years. Orwell would have been more pleased with another longtime Irish resident and contemporary of Swift, William Penn (1688–1718), who in some ways was a bigger man than Swift and whose political and religious pronouncements with respect to Pennsylvania show him to be well ahead of his times. This means that Swift could not be, and certainly was not, a front-line popularizer, arguing in his sermons for the existence of an all-loving God and in his political writings insisting on the rights (as Orwell would have done) of all the people on his distressed island. In truth, the ironic fact is that this Irish patriot of the eighteenth century was a spokesman of but one small segment of the people resident in Ireland. "What [Swift] overlooked is, to be sure, amazing to us today," wrote Ricardo Quintana; "for the native Irish were wholly excluded from his community of free men, and of the Anglo-Irish only those conforming to the Established Church [Swift's church] had full rights."[33] Thanks to Penn their "full rights" would be guaranteed in Pennsylvania, too. But then so would be everybody else's, there.

Swift's Old Age

Swift's last years are sometimes introduced by a reference to a story told by Edward Young. Looking at a dying elm tree, Swift is said to have declared, "I shall be like that tree, I shall die at the top."[34] The account of these final years commonly goes on to mention Samuel Johnson's remarkable declaration in "The Vanity of Human Wishes": "Swift expires a driv'ler and a show." Edward Young's report I have no reason to question, but Johnson's great line simply is not true. Professor Ehrenpreis remarks that "Swift was no more neurotic than Pope or Johnson, and probably less so. The tradition of his madness has been rejected for forty years by every qualified scholar who has bothered to look into the question."[35]

The facts of Swift's last years are for the most part the not unfamiliar facts about a man who grows old. On into the 1730s—Swift was then in his middle and late sixties—he worked at his job, presiding over chapter meetings at the deanery, listening carefully and critically to the sermons of young preachers in his cathedral, and performing his extensive charities.[36] Hawkesworth, referring to the years after 1724, writes that "Over the populace [Swift] was the most absolute monarch that ever governed men, and he was regarded by persons of every rank with veneration and esteem."[37] Such facts make fiction of the generally held beliefs about Swift's old age. In his seventieth year in a letter to Pope he said that, walking through the streets of Dublin, he received "a thousand hats and blessings."[38] These are not the words of, and that is not the reception given to, "a driv'ler and a show."

My own favorite story about these last years is one told by Sheridan, one of Swift's earliest and most interesting biographers. It seems that "a great rabble assembled . . . before the Deanery-door in Kevin street" in order to see an eclipse. Swift, apparently disturbed by the noise made by the people, sent for the beadle and instructed him to tell the crowd that "it is the Dean of St. Patrick's will and pleasure, that the eclipse be put off till this hour to-morrow." Sheridan adds: "The mob upon this notice immediately dispersed."[39]

But Swift increasingly in the late 1730s withdrew from society and lost contact with friends whom he had been intimate with for decades: Sheridan, Lady Acheson, and the Pilkingtons, for example.[40] Also, in addition to the vertigo and deafness associated with Ménière's disease, he began to suffer more and more from bad memory and poor eyesight. Clearly incapable of carrying on his normal duties, he appointed in 1739 a subdean to preside over meetings of the cathedral chapter.[41] In 1742 (at age seventy-five), Swift was put under the care of a committee of guardians—not because he was mad, but because, as Ehrenpreis points out, "it was the most convenient way for a senile person, living alone, to be defended against various sorts of exploitation."[42]

The remaining years of his life were very sad ones. He spoke little, and when told on his birthday in 1743 that Dubliners were again going to celebrate the event with bonfires and illuminations, he said, "It is all folly, they had better let it alone."[43] In 1745 he died, and the bells of his own cathedral were rung, mournfully because muffled, for four days. Crowds of people came to the deanery to pay their respects to their friend there in his own hall where he was laid out. Sir Walter Scott reports that "Young and old of all ranks surrounded the house, to pay the last tribute of sorrow and affection. Locks of hair were . . . eagerly sought after. . . ."[44] In fact, when the attendant sitting by the coffin had briefly to leave for a time, she returned to find that someone had cut off one of those locks. "After that day," as Monck Mason reports, "no person was admitted to see the body."[45]

Swift was buried, near Stella, in St. Patrick's Cathedral, beneath the famous Latin epitaph that he himself had composed: "*Hic depositum est Corpus / Jonathon Swift, . . . ubi saeva Indignatio / Ulterious / Cor lacerare nequit / Abi Viator / Et imitare, si poteris, / Strenuum pro virili / Libertatis Vindicatorem.*" ("Here lies the body of Jonathan Swift . . . where savage indignation can no more lacerate his heart. Go, traveller, and imitate if you can one who strove with all his strength to champion liberty.")

In his own way, Swift did serve human liberty. However, this ideal of service—combined with his lifelong alertness to any form of pomposity and sentimentality, and his sardonic vision of reality—seems less well expressed by his epitaph than by the major legacy in his will: he left money to establish, "in or near Dublin," a hospital for "ideots and lunaticks," because, as he said in his own "Verses on the Death of Dr. Swift," "No Nation wanted [that is, *needed*] it so much."

The Best of Jonathan Swift, the Writer

For almost half a century, Jonathan Swift was a writer. During these years he wrote a great deal—in fact, an astonishing amount when we consider that writing was not his main occupation. Herbert Davis's great Shakespeare Head edition of *The Prose Works of Jonathan Swift* includes thirteen volumes (minus the index); the edition by Sir Harold Williams of Swift's poetry embraces three volumes and of his correspondence five volumes; another two volumes make up the Williams edition of Swift's *Journal to Stella*.

Looking at this extensive body of writing, Herbert Read comments: "All that Swift wrote is empirical, experiencial, *actuel*." It is impossible to detach it from circumstances; we must consider each book or pamphlet in relation to its political intention."[46] With the first part of this quotation I can agree immediately because anything that anybody writes is apt in one sense or another to be "empirical, experiencial, *actuel*." With the second part of the quotation I have trouble, however, for in the first place, Swift wrote a number of things that quite clearly have little or no "political intention." I think at once of the many poems to Stella; of the pamphlet entitled *A Proposal for Correcting, Improving and Ascertaining the English Tongue* (1712); of the *Letter to a Young Gentleman Lately Entered into Holy Orders* (1720); or of the *Letter to a Young Lady on Her Marriage* (1723). Of much greater concern to me, however, is an assertion that "It is impossible to detach [any work by Swift] from circumstances. . . ." Mr. Read does qualify his position somewhat with the remark that, "though none of Swift's works can be separated from its historical occasion, historical considerations cannot usurp aesthetic judgement."[47] However, my inclination would be to rephrase the sentence this way: "Of course aesthetic judgment must not be usurped; moreover, the emphatic testimony of the centuries is that such judgments are very generally made without much regard for historical considerations." Therefore, for almost three hundred years readers have been quietly separating Swift's works from the circumstances that produced them. In fact, if a work is seriously enfeebled (that is, it does not mean much to the reader) when removed from the circumstances that produced it, the work is not much read. This has been the fate by and large, alas, of *The Drapier Letters,* of the essays in the *Examiner,* and of *The Conduct of the Allies.* Really not much of what is usually called "background" knowledge is needed to bring these works to life and make them instructive and even on occasion a delight to read. But at least some special knowledge is needed; the result is that for each reader of *The Drapier Letters,* there are, I would suppose, ten thousand readers of *Gulliver's Travels,* a book that can be and usually is separated from its "historic occasion."

It is to be lamented that works such as *The Drapier Letters, The Conduct of the Allies,* and the *Examiner* are neglected. However, it is apparently one of the laws of literary survival: the book that cannot be "detached" from the "historic occasion" becomes a kind of dead monument, monumentally ignored. To survive, any form of art—a play, a poem, a novel, or a prose satire—must transcend its occasion and speak forcefully and eloquently to those who know little or nothing about the occasion. Some scholars are distressed that ignorance may cause a reader to give to a piece of literature a different reading from that intended by the author, or a reading that is even inappropriate to the "historic occasion" that produced it. However, since the passage of years makes such different or "wrong" readings inevitable, and since these "wrong" readings always offer at least the theoretical possibility of being an improvement on the reading originally intended and/or given, I suggest that we view these changes stoically and that, though we may sometimes sigh, we should never sob about the matter. Indeed the only real regret is that occasionally something very good suffers the fate of getting attention only from specialists.

With a few exceptions, the works that I analyze and assess in the following chapters have transcended the occasion that produced them. In that sense, they are "the best of Swift." To know something of the background of these great works is very often a tremendously revealing and enriching experience, and our attention to such background information is justified to the extent that it increases our pleasure in reading them. The danger is that the searching out and the analysis of background information may become in itself so major a concern that the literary work itself is either forgotten or unconsciously or even deliberately overlooked by critics who do not see the need for, or would actually be embarrassed by, any attempt to judge a piece of writing. This danger I have tried to avoid by keeping the literary work (the poem, the essay, the prose satire) always at the center of attention. And I have along with my analyses made many judgments; for it seems to me that analysis and assessment are and ought to be the very best bedfellows. As I have said, however, the scope of my discussion has by and large been limited to those magical creations, "the best of Swift," that have transcended the circumstances that gave them birth.

Chapter Two
"For the Universal Improvement of Mankind"

An Overview of the *Tale* Volume

Swift's first great prose work, *A Tale of a Tub*, was published in 1704 (though written at various times earlier) in a volume that was also to include *The Battle of the Books* and *The Mechanical Operation of the Spirit* (hereafter referred to as the *Tale* volume). Like most of his work, it was issued anonymously and earned Swift no money (it actually cost him money because it delayed and in fact came close to ruining his career in the church); and also like most of his work, it was, as the charming candor of the subtitle informs us, "Written for the Universal Improvement of Mankind."

Though Swift's authorship of the *Tale* volume is now generally accepted,[1] speculation about the author began immediately and continued for years. Swift's cousin, Thomas Swift, was a leading contender for the honors. Sir William Temple was mentioned as a possibility.[2] And even as late as 1762 Samuel Johnson said, as reported in Boswell's *Life of Johnson*, "I doubt that the 'Tale of a Tub' be [Swift's]; for he never owned it and it is much above his usual manner." Johnson made no mention of the fact that Swift's motivation for writing part of the *Tale* volume—namely *The Battle of the Books*—was to aid his patron, Sir William Temple, in a controversy between the "ancients" and the "moderns."

In his *Essay upon the Ancient and Modern Learning* (1690), Temple had upheld the superiority of the ancients. He attempted to refute what seemed to him to be the two essential arguments of the moderns: the first was that Nature, always constant, must produce genius as great today as yesterday or tomorrow; the second was that the moderns, profiting from the great store of riches in their heritage, must necessarily surpass the ancients. Émile Pons summarizes Temple's conclusion accurately and succinctly: "Our age has none of the greatness of ancient times. Even in the experimental sciences, where we think we are superior, we do not really compare. 'Has Harvey outdone Hippocrates, or Wilkins Archimedes?' " Pons then comments as follows: "Temple's complete incomprehension of the scientific discoveries of his day is characteristic and aids us in better understanding Swift's indifference. His admiration for the literature of the Ancients blocks his horizon. It prevents him not only from understanding his own times but also from differentiating what is truly admirable in antiquity from what is not. His admiration is thoroughly conventional and, because it is interwoven with error and superstition, he makes the famous mistake which was to bring him so much badgering."[3]

Temple's mistake occurred in his comment that "The two most ancient [books] that I know of in prose among those we call profane authors, are Aesop's Fables and Phalaris's Epistles, both living near the same time, which was that of Cyrus and Pythagoras." This error was not challenged by clever young William Wotton, the first of the moderns to reply to Temple. However, the error was dramatically and emphatically revealed in 1697 when Wotton issued a second edition of his *Reflections upon Ancient and Modern Learning,* which included Richard Bentley's *Dissertation on the Epistles of Phalaris.* Bentley, a great scholar, proved that the *Epistles of Phalaris* and the *Fables* were spurious. Phalaris could not have written the epistles with which he was credited because, among other reasons, they mention cities that were not even in existence during the life of Phalaris. Such a disclosure was a victory for the moderns. However, Richard Bentley had personally offended a young and well-born dilettante named Charles Boyle when the latter, as a student at Oxford, was asked to edit the *Epistles.* One essential manuscript necessary for him to complete his assignment was in the St. James's Library, the king's library where Bentley was keeper. Bentley did not seem to Boyle to be sufficiently helpful; therefore Boyle, later the earl of Orrery, was moved to comment publicly and ironically on "the singular humanity" (meaning of course "inhumanity") of Richard Bentley. Obviously modern learning was ill-mannered and needed chastisement; so this disclosure was a victory for the ancients.

The quarrel seems clearly to have bogged down on occasion into irrelevancies. Indeed, we should not be surprised that even Swift was apparently no more concerned about the central philosophical issues than we are today. Recall that, in college, "he did poorly in what he would always dislike—abstract philosophy and formal rhetoric."[4] However, there is no reason to doubt that what initially impelled him into the fray was mainly the understandable desire to support his patron and employer, Sir William Temple.

A Tale of a Tub was published in 1704 but, as mentioned above, it was written at various times earlier. How much earlier and what was written when are questions that can only in part be answered. A few dates may be be mentioned with some confidence: for example, the "Epistle Dedicatory" is subscribed 1697; the "Conclusion" has a reference to the *Histoire de M. Constance,* which Swift read in 1697,[5] so the "Conclusion" was very probably written at about that time. Perhaps he had even sketched out the nub of his whole story, or had written some parts of it—maybe the religious allegory—when he was a student at Trinity College.[6] Swift himself does not help as much with this problem, except that he does say, in the "Apology" inserted in the 1710 edition of the *Tale,* that "The greatest part of that book was finished above thirteen years since, 1696, which is eight years before it was published."

In my study the dates are not of crucial importance, though I believe that they do suggest something about Swift's frame of mind when he wrote this volume. It looks as though he was in his late twenties or maybe even younger when he began writing. In 1686 he graduated from Trinity College. He was ordained priest in 1695 and awarded the miserable little parish in Kilroot, in northern (and Presbyterian) Ireland. In 1696 he returned, again, to Sir William and to a subservient position, again, as Temple's secretary. At this point he was really not much better off than he had been ten years earlier, though he was still full of hopes for some kind of preferment. In 1699 Temple died, having done nothing for the proud dependent who had served him. Subsequently, in 1707, after he had made some other false starts, the Anglican Church in Ireland sent him to England to seek remission of the First Fruits from Queen Anne. Courted by the Whigs, he labored in their causes and, again, got nothing. When the Tories came to power in 1710, he saw hopes for help with the First Fruits problem. He joined with the Tories; the First Fruits were remitted; but Swift got no credit. So it went, again and again. Always there were the hopes that something good would come his way. Nothing that he really wanted ever did. Is it any wonder, then, that some pages of his writing during these frustrating years—writing that included *The Battle of the Books* and *A Tale of a Tub*—reflect such bitterness and despair?

Of more importance than establishing the dates is the question of the subject matter, and on this point we have some help. The author himself announces his subject as "abuses in Religion" and in "Learning." Thus, if we accept his near-enough guess about the date (1696) as the year when he finished "the greatest part" of the *Tale,* then we may not unreasonably assume that he put aside this work in 1697 to help Temple by writing *The Battle of the Books* as a satire on the moderns—especially on the false learning of the moderns. This task completed, but the work for some reason remaining in manuscript form[7]—it may have been that Temple, who was not overly fond of satire, advised against publication—Swift returned to his *Tale* and its religious allegory.

At this point, perhaps as Ricardo Quintana sees it, he realized that corruptions in learning (the announced subject of the *Battle*) and in religion (the announced subject of the *Tale*) have a common denominator[8]—irrationality being the cause of both—and so he put his two books between one set of covers. He then dovetailed his *Battle* and the *Tale* by the use of the so-called digressions (actually thematic tenons from the *Battle*) that attacked false learning—"A Digression Concerning Critics," "A Digression in the Modern Kind," etc.—and added the section entitled *The Mechanical Operation of the Spirit,* which is a sort of spinoff from the talk about Jack in section 11 of the *Tale.* There appears to have been no particular logic in the order of these digressions, a fact that may perhaps be surmised from the remark at the close of section 7: "The necessity of this digression will easily excuse the length; and I have chosen for it as proper a place as I could readily find. If the judicious reader can assign a fitter, I do here empower him to remove it into any other corner he pleases." Irony? Simple whimsy? It is impossible to tell, one way or the other, though I suspect irony.

In any event, these conjectures about the conposition of the *Tale* are consistent with the aforementioned comment in the "Apology" to the *Tale,* where Swift declares his plan: "the Abuses in Religion, he proposed to set forth in the Allegory of the Coats, and the three Brothers, which was to make up the body of the discourse. Those in Learning he chose to introduce by way of digressions." Swift also may have sensed that the narrator who pretended to be the author of the *Battle,* and of the digressions, and of *The Mechanical Operation of the Spirit* was a type fortunately not inconsistent with the Grub Street hack who pretended to be the author of the *Tale.* Thus, with a single basic theme and with what looks to some people like a single narrator to give a semblance of consistency to the tone and the point of view, he was enabled to make one book from the various parts he had started with. But these conjectures must be most cautiously advanced since they cannot in any sense be proved. It must be allowed, however, that the ironic comment in section 5 of the *Tale* reads very much like Swift's confession of his own method in this book: "I have known some authors [who] enclose digressions in one another, like a nest of boxes." The "nest of boxes" is an apt description for the surprising and intricate volume that he bequeathed to us in 1704 and then again in his edition of 1710.

A work accomplished in the way that Swift accomplished the *Tale* volume almost inevitably lacks a degree of unity and cohesion. As a consequence it is no surprise to hear Guthkelch and Smith say, "After two centuries of annotation [the book] still has its puzzles in plenty."[9] One reason among many reasons that the volume succeeds as well as it does, however, and one reason that it can be read as a book with a beginning, a middle, and an end, is explained by Pons's interesting conjecture that Swift turned to his manuscript—adding to it and editing it—when he found his inspiration and his temperament tuned to a certain, and generally the same, key.[10] The book would have achieved a more obvious unity and would no doubt have pleased more readers if, to shift the metaphor, the author had been more expert at the mortise and tenon work necessary to make one book out of many parts. He was not interested in this art: not unexpectedly, therefore, we witness here, as in other of Swift's works, a number of irrelevancies, inconsistencies, and paradoxes.

Nor was Swift expert in the handling of his narrator, the so-called hack. This hack, a figure made familiar to us by Ronald Paulson,[11] is most useful when there is a clear distinction between his "voice," which mouths absurdities, and Swift's "voice," which of course is altogether different. But it does not always work this way. J. A. Downie claims that, "If the Hack is not a full-blown *persona,* then he is the mouthpiece for Swift—he *may* at times speak Swift's mind, but we can never be sure."[12] Though this caution must always be remembered, I believe that sometimes we really can be quite sure. Consider, for example, the very clear implications of the imagery in this little catechism in section 2 of the *Tale:* "[What] is man himself but a micro-coat, or rather a complete suit of clothes with all its trimmings. . . . [T]hose things, which the world calls improperly suits of clothes are in reality the most refined species of animals. . . . Is it not they who walk the streets, fill up parliament-, play-, bawdy-houses. . . . If one of them is trimmed up with a good chain, and a red gown, and a white rod, and a great

horse, it is called a Lord-Mayor. . . ." This famous clothes-imagery
seems to say that man's predicament is not the result of the abuse of his
reason; rather it has come about because he has no reason at all. He is
not even a man. He is more like, if we care to meditate about it, a
clothed broomstick: brainless and therefore no more capable of thought
than an animal. Is it the hack who tells us this? I doubt it. The voice
sounds to me remarkably like Swift's and I think that it is Swift's, even
if Mr. Downie is not sure.

But Downie's caution reveals one of the many critical cruxes in the
Tale volume. The line between the hack's voice and Swift's is so often
blurred that it is quite understandable why some readers would conclude that we never can be certain about *who* is talking. There are
others—Émile Pons, Herbert Davis, and John Traugott come to
mind—who take a different approach: "We *know* perfectly well," Traugott writes, "[when] we are in the presence of Swift."[13]

Pons and Traugott, moreover, do not confine Swift's satire in the
Tale volume to the more tidy thematic lines that Paulson and Quintana
do. Pons, in his classic study (1925) *Swift, les années de jeunesse et le
"Conte du Tonneau"* (*Swift's Early Years and His "Tale of a Tub"*), suggested that in his *Tale* volume Swift went way beyond his stated
intention—to satirize abuses in religion and in learning—and that it
was this "going beyond" that got him into trouble with Queen Anne
and with other very powerful forces in both England and Ireland. Pons
believed that at some of the highest points in the *Tale,* Swift's imagination put his satire into conflict with beliefs that he would ordinarily be
expected to hold,[14] like a belief in the sacraments of his own church;
moreover, in his use of certain mythical and symbolic images (for
example, that man is but a hollow suit of clothes, filled with wind and
vapors), Swift was not able "to curb a way of thinking which by this
myth . . . liberated itself and . . . knew its essential form."[15] Consistent with this belief, Pons had no problem deciding whose voice is to
be heard in the passage beginning, "What is man himself but a micro-
coat, or rather a complete suit of clothes . . . ?" Swift said it; his satire
having been "liberated" by his imagery, he paradoxically enunciated a
point of view totally at odds with that of the church he served.

More recently John Traugott has made substantially some of the
same points that Pons had made more than half a century earlier. For
example Traugott tells us that "Whenever one of [Swift's] mad or idiot
figures begins to spin fantastic symbols and allegories, [he] is discovering his own truths. The guise is the way to freedom for [this] proper

priest."[16] Again, from Traugott: "The satire [in *The Mechanical Operation of the Spirit*] does not fall back upon the fool but the fool is the agent by which Swift freed his imagination and gave vent to his deepest thoughts."[17] The use of the persona "freed" the priest (Swift) from any obligation to his conventional, priestly attitudes. Hiding behind this persona he became free, it would appear, to denounce in fact just about everything a priest is presumed to believe in. But if the persona *is* Swift, as some people thought then and some do now, then it is incredible that poor Jonathan Swift rose as high in the church as he eventually did.

At this point my intention is to initiate a fairly detailed examination of the *Tale* volume. I shall refer to critics like Pons and Traugott, when such references seem appropriate. But my comments will also rely heavily on Ronald Paulson's concept about the hack-narrator and Ricardo Quintana's thesis that the *Tale* volume has a single satiric purpose. Further, since emphasis will fall on Swift's book as a whole, my principal task will be to discover the nature of the contribution that some of the principal parts make to the whole of this astonishing work.

A *Tale of a Tub* (Part 1)

As books go, *A Tale of a Tub* is not big. For example, *Gulliver's Travels* is more than half again as long. Despite its comparative brevity, however, Swift thought highly of his book. Sir Walter Scott records the famous story about how Swift, reading the *Tale* many years after its publication, was moved to exclaim: "Good God, what a genius I had when I wrote that book."[18] Admittedly, alas, this genius wrote a book that was somewhat flawed; and this particular genius could on occasion be something of a bore, particularly when his wit became joyless and needlessly hyperbolic. Recall Jack, who "had a tongue so musculous and subtile, that he could twist it up into his nose" (section 11): hyperbole and hardly very funny. Pons, refusing to admire such passages, settled for calling them "labored puerilities" that "defeat the satiric thrust of his satire."[19] Or recall in the *Battle* the goddess Momus taking the ugliest of her monsters, "full glutted from her spleen, and [flinging] it invisibly into [Wotton's] mouth, which, flying straight up into his head, squeezed out his eye-balls. . . ." Yet having endured more than enough of this unsavory type of thing, most readers would nonetheless agree with Swift's own judgment. Despite its faults, this book is the work of a genius. Not only is it a brilliant young man's romp—in places one of the most hilarious in literature—it is also in many parts an angry, an unforgettable, and a still relevant satire.

Little happens in the early pages of the *Tale.* What the reader finds is, first, a list of treatises "wrote by" the same author; then, in some editions, "An Analytical Table" (which we may skip, as it is not Swift's); then, added to the 1710 edition, "An Apology"; then a little "Postscript to the Apology"; then the "Dedication to Lord Somers" (an early demonstration of Swift's great talent for the backhanded compliment); then "The Bookseller to The Reader"; then "The Epistle Dedicatory to Prince Posterity"; and finally a "Preface" that adumbrates in one way or another most of the themes that the whole book will deal with. But the narrator appears even yet to be in no hurry, for after the "Preface" comes the "Introduction"; and only after this section does the story commence. It begins, all innocence, with "Once upon a time. . . ." What gall this writer has! All in all, he gives us six parts to the 1704, and seven parts to the 1710, edition; *then* he begins, as though he were beginning a bedtime story for children.

Only an unreflecting reader could possibly be duped by Swift's tease. Actually, the book gets under way with one of its major themes—the satire on modern learning—on its very first page. There, in the fashion of "modern" scholarship, the author announces his credentials, so to say, for speaking as an authority. He has published nothing; but with great glibness he tells of his list of treatises "which will be speedily published." The list includes such absurd works as "A General History of Ears," "A Modest Defence of the Proceedings of the Rabble . . ." and so on—eleven titles in all. The straight-faced whimsy is followed by the parody—for that is what it is—of all the elaborate and ridiculous paraphernalia with which we are to assume a truly scholarly work begins. But as it is frequently with Swift, the joke is on us, for after all this "scholarly" build-up preparing us for the reading of a scholarly book, the story commences with "Once upon a time. . . ."

Though by no means dominant, this sort of impish wit is, happily, met with frequently. One deft trick was the use of William Wotton's notes for the 1710 edition of the *Tale,* the one now generally used. Wotton had written a reply (*Observations upon The Tale of a Tub*) in opposition to Swift's *Tale.* So, when the 1710 edition was being prepared for the press, Swift, to get back at his adversary, coolly stole from Wotton's book remarks for Benjamin Tooke, Swift's printer, to use as explanatory footnotes. [20] The victim's reactions to such a piece of impudence have not been recorded. In this whole episode Swift's ironic voice is clearly heard behind that of his hack, the so-called tale teller: the learned book may not have anything at all to say, but it will have lots of prefaces and, of course, many footnotes, some of which are pretty silly.

It is probably wise, though I believe not essential, to see our supposed narrator gradually identifying himself in the early pages of the *Tale* volume. Also, especially for the discovery of Swift's many uses of irony, it is always helpful to try to distinguish between the real (Swift) and the purported "author" (the persona or hack or, another name for him, "the Grubean sage"). Whether this narrator is the same throughout the volume and whether he is a consistent and fully realized character are matters that have already been commented upon and will be commented upon again. However, it is in the prefatory sections that readers speak of first meeting this purported "author." Appearing initially in his own person in "The Epistle Dedicatory to Prince Posterity," he proves to be a modern who is astonished that anyone "should have Assurance in the face of the Sun, to go about persuading Your Highness [Posterity] that our Age is almost wholly illiterate and has hardly produc'd one Writer upon any Subject." The two voices that produce the irony are here completely distinct. The apparent meaning of the passage is voiced by our sincere though obtuse hack; the real meaning is voiced by Swift. Ignoring for the moment how many good modern writers he knew, and thinking only of the prodigious amount of trash being published, he may be presumed to have said something like this: "Exactly so. Our age has produced hardly one real writer, and certainly none from among your crowd of hackwriters." The same sort of irony appears just a few pages later, when the "author" makes a comment that Swift's voice flatly contradicts: "There is a Person styl'd Dr. B——tl——y [Bentley]," the narrator reports, "who has written near a thousand Pages of immense Erudition, giving a full and true Account of a certain Squabble. . . . He is a Writer of infinite Wit and Humour." As we know, Swift in fact despised Bentley and all he wrote.

Our narrator has written "Four score and eleven Pamphlets . . . under three Reigns, and for the Service of six and thirty Factions" (see "Introduction" in the *Tale*); and now, in the throes of writing this *Tale* volume, he resides in a garret. He tells us that "the shrewdest pieces of this treatise were conceived in a garret" ("Preface"). In section 6 of the *Tales* he calls himself "a true modern." On the record, then, he appears to be a fairly typical "modern hack writer." When he does finally get to his task of telling a tale about a tub ("Once upon a time . . . "), he straightway interrupts with "A Digression in the Modern Kind" in which he mournfully confesses that "it is lamentable to behold, with what a lazy scorn many of the yawning readers in our age, do now-a-days twirl over forty or fifty pages of preface and dedication (which is the usual modern stint), as if it were so much Latin." This complaint (perfectly applicable to what he is doing) aired, the hack "happily" resumes his subject, "to the infinite satisfaction both of the reader and the author."

But the subject is not resumed for long. Soon comes "A Digression in Praise of Digressions." This digression completed, the narrator remarks upon his "return, with great alacrity" to his tale. Alas, he simply cannot stay with it. He teeters wildly off—though, of course, Swift sees to it that thematically he is still very much "on"—with the climax of his book: Swift calls it "A Digression Concerning Madness." Here indeed in this sequence is a wantonly insane parody of what modern learning and its abuses have come to.

The Battle of the Books

The comic aspects of *A Tale of a Tub* are integral to Swift's attack on false learning. This attack is in turn reinforced in *The Battle of the Books*, particularly by the central episode in that section, the fable of the spider and the bee.

The Battle of the Books is of only slight historical import in a controversy that for a time aroused deep and fierce antagonisms. Something of the nature of this controversy can be realized from a look at one of its famous high points, a few years earlier. On 27 January 1687 Charles Perrault read to the French Academy "Le siècle de Louis le Grand." This poem contained such lines as "Je vois les anciens, sans plier les genous; / ils sont grands, il est vrai, mais hommes comme nous" (Though I admire the ancient writers, I am not going to worship them. It is true that they are great; but like us, they are also human). The French poet's words are so entirely reasonable to twentieth-century ears that we are apt to forget how inevitable would be the conflict until this issue was either resolved or ceased to be of serious concern to anybody. In Swift's day, the issue was still of vital importance to great numbers of people.

We need no reminder that Swift's part in the controversy does more credit to his heart than to his head. As a philosophic contribution, his share is of no worth except unintentionally and insofar as his imagery suggests the trivial nature of the quarrel. He sided with the ancients—

and with his patron. At the same time, in real life he knew and admired the writings of Addison, Arbuthnot, Gay, and Pope—to mention only a few eminent moderns of his day. It is thus obvious that his concern in this historic quarrel was less to ridicule the moderns than it was merely to chastise those men who opposed his patron. The truth of this possibility is buttressed by the fact that some of the best fun and most effective ridicule is not particularly relevant to the issue supposedly at stake. When Virgil ("the brave Ancient") is about to be engaged in combat and his adversary lifts the visor of his armor, Virgil "suddenly started," for the visor does not reveal a face. "The Ancient" has to look deep into the cavernous depths of the helmet, which is "nine times too large" for its owner, to locate the tiny head of the man who is offering to do battle with him. The head, we discover, is that of Dryden, whose famous translation of *Virgil* had appeared in 1696. Here is laughter, all right. But to call "Cousin" Dryden a "pinhead" is not to argue seriously for the central thesis here involved. So, too, as Pons observed, the satire on the very first page of the *Battle* is directed not against the moderns but against "dogs" of all kinds,[21] ancient and modern.

The first page of the *Battle,* like the first page of *Gulliver's Travels,* deserves more attention than it usually gets. Swift writes, "For, to speak in the phrase of writers upon the politics, we may observe in the Republic of Dogs (which, in its original, seems to be an institution of the many) . . . that civil broils arise among them when it happens for one great bone to the seized on by some leading dog. . . ." These significant words tell us that while Swift was saying one thing, his imagery said something else. Though we cannot much doubt the sincerity of the support he gave to his patron and to the ancients, the imagery suggests that he really cared nothing whatsoever about this silly quarrel. He was far above it, looking down on the squabbling "Republic of Dogs." He thus unwittingly but quite decisively undercut what were presumed to be his reasons for supporting the ancients. "War," as the very first sentence on the first page of the *Battle* insists, "is the child of pride." If this be so, then this particular little war was absurd. And Boyle, Bentley, Wotton, and even Temple himself—dogs, all of them.

Swift's real though unconscious contempt for both sides in the quarrel is effectively and characteristically wrapped up in the familiar comparison of man to animal. Émile Pons, who made a special province out of the investigation of this comparison, says that, to Swift, "Humanity is as depraved as the most contemptible kinds of animals (Man is very likely in Swift's later writings to become sometimes even worse than these animals). From now on [Pons is referring to the time when the *Battle* was written] this comparison of Man and Animal is fixed permanently in Swift's imagination. The link between the two is never to be broken. It . . . will remain a constant factor in his work."[22]

Indeed, the symbol is pervasive. Two instances: the first shows Swift using the symbol to comment corrosively on Bentley and Wotton. This comment appears toward the end of the *Battle,* where the moderns are compared to "two mongrel curs, whom native greediness and domestic want provoke and join in partnership, though fearful, nightly to invade the folds of some rich grazier, . . . [They] creep soft and slow . . . , nor dare they bark . . . , but one surveys the region round, while t'other scouts the plain, if haply to discover, at distance from the flock, some carcass half devoured, the refuse of gorged wolves, or ominous ravens."

But the fable of the spider and the bee, the second instance, is the outstanding demonstration of Swift's employment of Pons's "le mythe animal" in the *Battle.* In this episode we learn that there once dwelt in the library of St. James[23] a certain spider, "swollen up to the first magnitude by the destruction of an infinite number of flies." One Friday, into this spider's web flew a bee, who was temporarily entrapped. Having to his own great satisfaction extricated himself, the bee becomes engaged in conversation with the spider, who is understandably quite angry at the damage done to his web:

"A plague split you," said he, "for a giddy son of a whore, . . . Do you think I have nothing else to do, in the devil's name, but to mend and repair after your arse?"

"Good words, friend," said the bee. . . . I'll give you my hand and word to come near your kennel no more. . . ."

The conversation between the spider (symbolizing the moderns in this "Battle") and the bee (the ancients) ends with the bee's remark:

"Your inherent portion of dirt does not fail of acquisitions, by sweepings exhaled from below; and one insect furnishes you with a share of poison to destroy another. So that, in short, the question comes all to this—whether is the nobler being of the two, that which, by a lazy contemplation of four inches round, by an overweening pride, feeding and engendering on itself, turns all into excrement and venom, producing nothing at all, but flybane and a cobweb; or that which, by an universal range, with long search, much study, true judgement, and distinction of things, brings home honey and wax."

Aesop, overhearing this debate from his position in his book on the
library shelf, makes the comment that reinforces the bee's position and
gets to the heart of the matter:

"As for us the Ancients, we are content with the bee to pretend to nothing of
our own, beyond our wings and our voice, that is to say our flights and our
language. For the rest, whatever we have got, has been by infinite labour and
search, and ranging through every corner of nature; the difference is, that,
instead of dirt and poison, we have chosen to fill our hives with honey and
wax, thus furnishing mankind with the two noblest of things, which are
sweetness and light."

The bee in this fable is a fairly elegant fellow who must have given
pleasure to Temple, himself a beekeeper.[24] Swift probably got him
from Temple's essay "Of Poetry" (and Temple himself probably read of
him in Bacon). The dirty, vulgar, but vibrant spider was added by
Swift, and, because it is used for satiric purposes, evidences Swift's
more characteristic employment of the animal, or to be quite literally
exact, here the insect myth.

The fable of the spider and the bee makes an unforgettable impact on
the reader. This effect is fortunate for, if we consider the whole *Battle* as
exposition or as argument, we must see its confusions and inconsistencies. In these respects, this work does more credit to Swift's heart, as I
have suggested above, than to his head. (The fact that he had a heart is,
of course, a healthy reminder to students who have not read Swift's
biography very carefully.[25]) However, far more significant than the
favorable impact of this episode is the fact that the story of the spider
and the bee almost, and quite miraculously, shades out discordant
notes and brings wonderfully into focus all the elements that give
abiding value to the satire of the *Battle*.[26] Thus the value of the satire
remains where, happily, its force has always been strongest anyway.
That is, in addition to supporting Sir William Temple by making sport
of the moderns who had attacked him, the *Battle* does make a notable
statement about false learning.

Best read, I think this book satirizes pretense: learning that is false
because, though footnotes and prefaces give it a form, it is entirely
lacking in substance. So long as learned pomposity, surely pedantry,
bootlicking opportunism, and sterile scholarship (all mere dirty "webs"
of dirty "spiders") still abide here and there, so long as "mongrel curs"
continue to haunt our bowers of learning, Swift's comments in the

Battle and in the digressions of the *Tale* will remain sharply relevant. True learning, ancient or modern, "brings home honey and wax"; and it ministers to mankind with "sweetness and light."

A Tale of a Tub (Part 2)

In "An Apology," which is the first sustained prose in the 1710 edition of *A Tale of a Tub,* Swift commented on his dual satiric purpose and also on this method of composition: "The Abuses in Religion, he proposed to set forth in the Allegory of the Coats, and the three Brothers, which was to make up the body of the discourse. Those in Learning he chose to introduce by way of digressions." The satire on Learning I have already discussed; it remains now to remark upon (1) the abuses in religion, and (2) the combining of the two satiric themes under the single heading, which is the irrationality common to them both.

Swift in his "Preface" explains the basis for the *Tale.* When threatened by a whale, sailors fling a tub from the ship, "to divert [the whale] from laying violent hands [*sic*] upon the ship." The "ship in danger" is, as the narrator points out, "the commonwealth." The "dangers" were probably restricted, originally, to Swift's idea of the abuses then most current in religion. Later, as previously noted, these were mortised together with passages depicting abuses in learning—a union harmonious enough, at least thematically, if we consider that the two were, after all, very much alike. In all probability Swift had in mind other meanings of "a tale of a tub," common in his times: what people today might call "a tall tale" or "a cock-and-bull story." Also, in Swift's era dissenting preachers, like his own Jack the quack, sometimes stood upon a tub to preach. From this cluster of meanings, all of which he may have had at least vaguely in mind, an appropriately ironic proclamation may be constructed: "Here is a cock-and-bull story related by a quack for the good of the commonwealth!"

The classic opening line ("Once upon a time . . .") that begins innumerable other made-up stories is followed by an allegory about a father (Christ) who had three sons: Peter (the Roman Catholic Church); Martin (the Church of England); and Jack (the various sects of Protestant dissenters). Dying, the father left a will (the New Testament) and for each of his sons a new coat (the Church). His last commands were that the coats should not be altered and that the brothers should live together "like brethren and friends." From this point on there develops

an all too accurate allegory of Christian church history. Just as members
of the infant church of the first century were faced almost immediately
with the problems of worldliness, of "keeping up with the Joneses" and
"running with the crowd," so were the three youthful brothers in the
allegory. To keep abreast of their fashionable friends, they want at one
time to wear the shoulder knots that were then so popular. They
consult their father's will to see if they are allowed to decorate their
coats in this fashion. The will at no point says anything about so
important a matter, so the puzzled brothers for a moment do not know
what to do next. They are saved, however, when they hit upon the
ingenious device of picking out letters in the will, an "s" here, an "h"
there, and so on. In no time they have what they want: S,H,O,U,L,
D,E,R C,N,O,T,S. The "C" in CNOTS will serve very well for the
"K," especially since they cannot find a "K." Thus, "all farther difficulty [having] vanished," the brothers now wear whatever they want
to, whenever they want to. And thus their father's will (the word of
God) is perverted. At the same time, the brothers fall to quarrelling;
and since residence in one house (the one body of Christ) does not
content them, they separate. In fact, Peter "very fairly kicks" both his
brothers out of doors, ignoring their father's directive in the will: "you
should live together in one house."

The characterizations of the three brothers emerge more fully as this
narrative doggedly slogs its way through the many digressions. Mad
Jack, the dissenter, is hardly a likeable sort, but he is at least a lively
character. Peter, most readers agree, is not successfully drawn.[27] Martin is certainly not a very engaging sort, but he is at any rate a sensible
person. As a Church of England man, he is an integral part of that
"Commonwealth" that Swift's "tub" was desirous of protecting. It is
obvious that the reader is expected to accept him as the sane middle-of-
the-roader, as the good norm from which both Peter and Jack stray.
Theoretically, then, this reasonable and appealing norm will contrast
favorably with the uninviting, unintelligent, and hurtful ways of those,
like Peter and Jack, who for one senseless reason or another wander off
the track. Unfortunately, few readers find that Martin does a very good
job of making the Church of England attractive. John Traugott has
said, "That the *Tale* 'celebrates the Church of England as the most
perfect of all others in discipline and doctrine' is patently absurd—
unless we are to believe that what is *celebrated* is insipid, without force
or vitality."[28]

Swift's technique was applied more effectively in section 6, in which, alluding allegorically to the Reformation, he distinguishes between the three treatments given to the finery that each of the brothers had added to their coats. Peter (Roman Catholicism) had by this time added so much lace, fringe, and embroidery and so many ribbons and points that "there was hardly a thread of the original coat [the original church] to be seen." He liked it that way. Jack (dissenter Protestantism) so ripped and tore at the added finery that he looked "like a fresh Tenant of Newgate . . . or like a Bawd in her old Velvet-Petticoat." He, in effect, destroyed the coat. Martin, who took the middle course, removed all that he could, the while resolving "in no Case whatsoever, that the Substance of the Stuff should suffer injury." Again, in section 6, there is the assumption that Martin holds a reasonable middle course between two extremist brothers, basically similar in that "the phrenzy and the spleen of both have the same foundation."

But however, or even if, Swift may initially have intended to proportion his remarks among Peter, Martin, and Jack so that Martin would always be favorably situated in the middle, it is dissenting Jack who gets most of the attention, who is pursued most ferociously in the satire, and who comes most alive—even if only as a caricature of the dissenters Swift had met during his unhappy months in Kilroot. He discharges against Jack the whole tired arsenal of epithets that mankind seemingly never wearies of using to describe "those others" who are members of a religious minority of any sort, anywhere, any place. Indeed, they were already ancient epithets when Swift picked them up.[29] Ben Johnson, in a play he wrote almost a century earlier, had used very much the same arsenal, even then of vintage brand, to attack his Puritan character, Zeal-of-the-land-Busy. So Jack it is, says Swift, "whose intellectuals were overturned"; it is Jack who introduced a new deity, "by some called Babel, by others Chaos"; Jack "was brimful of Zeal"; Jack "brayed" like an ass. In truth, Thackeray's description, in his *The English Humourists of the Eighteenth Century,* of the final chapters of *Gulliver's Travels* applies much more aptly to Swift's Jack: "past all sense of manliness and shame, filthy in word, filthy in thought, furious, raging, obscene."

The climax of the *Tale* comes in section 9, entitled a "Digression concerning the Original, the Use and Improvement of Madness in a Commonwealth." It is a formidable and incredible and unforgettable account in which our Grub Street hack asks the reader to accept the fantastic premise that man's best recourse is not to his reason, but to madness. From this "commonsensical" first principle Swift, speaking through and sometimes I believe in place of his narrator, proceeds with glaring clarity to examine the real meaning of the serenity accruing to men victimized by delusion:

For the brain in its natural position . . . disposeth its owner to pass his life in the common forms, without any thoughts of subduing multitudes to his own power, his reasons, or his visions; and the more he shapes his understanding by the pattern of human learning, the less he is inclined to form parties after his particular notions, because that instructs him in his private infirmities, as well as in the stubborn ignorance of the people.

Who among us would willingly choose to pass our lives "in common forms"? Surely it is more interesting to subdue multitudes to our power, our reasons, or our visions. That is what we perhaps fancy. Swift continues:

But when man's fancy gets astride of his reason; when imagination is at cuffs with the senses, and common understanding, as well as common sense, is kicked out of doors; the first proselyte he makes is himself. . . .
. . . .
Those entertainments and pleasures we most value in life are such as dupe and play the wag with the senses. For if we take an examination of what is generally understood by happiness as it has respect either of the understanding or the senses, we shall find all its properties and adjuncts will herd under this short definition: that it is a perpetual possession of being well-deceived.
. . . .
Is any student [in Bedlam] tearing his straw in piece-meal, swearing and blaspheming, biting his grate, foaming at the mouth, and emptying his piss-pot in the spectator's face? Let the right worshipful the commissioners of inspection give him a regiment of dragoons, and send him into Flanders among the rest [of the soldiers].

As Émile Pons remarks, the above passage "absolutely eliminates any distinction between man and animal."[30] In hymning the sovereign animality of man, its thrust is not against corruption in religion and in learning. Here there is no religion; no learning.

[In Bedlam is a man] gravely taking the dimensions of his kennel, a person of foresight and insight. . . . He walks duly in one pace, entreats your penny with due gravity and ceremony, talks much of hard times, and taxes, and the whore of Babylon, bars up the wooden window of his cell constantly at eight o'clock, dreams of fire, and shoplifters, and court-customers, and privileged places. Now, what a figure would all these acquirements amount to, if the owner were sent to the city among his brethren!

The hack admits that, like the inmates of Bedlam, he is himself wont to let his reason be usurped by his imagination. If it is indeed the hack who wrote these words, he has written a devastating piece of self-criticism, the point of which has of course entirely escaped him.

Another astonishing and memorable demonstration of Swift's genius and of the terrifying consequences of irrationality is the brief account, in this same digression, of the woman who was flayed. "Last week," the hack's account reads, "I saw a woman flayed, and you will hardly believe how much it altered her person for the worse." Is a reader supposed to conclude from this that for cosmetic reasons only it is a good idea to avoid being flayed? A flaying does, after all, alter a person's appearance. Is it presumed that we should be surprised by this fact and indeed "hardly believe it"? How absurd our hack is. What a monster! How casually he ignores the central fact of the agony endured by this woman. It is undeniably valuable to flay away at the surface of things and so get to the substance—to the reality behind the appearance. But only a cruelly irrational and in fact insane narrator would use this method to get at the reality he seeks and then in his report of that appalling experience give us only the single fact that the woman looked rather the worse for it.

Our hack continues with an account of another episode in much the same vein: "Yesterday I ordered the carcass of a beau [a fashionable man-about-town] to be stripped in my presence. . . . I laid open his brain, his heart, and his spleen" and discovered all the faults (the reality) that the clothes and the skin had hidden. "[T]he defects increase . . . in number and bulk." There are right and humane ways of getting at the truth; but there are also insane ways. In the methods here reported—flaying a woman and dissecting a beau—there is madness.

Truly, as Martin Price says, "It is the special gift of the Tale Teller to be able to reach a damaging conclusion with no discomposure. . . ."[31] The comment, with its emphasis on "the Tale Teller" (our hack) returns us to a critical crux noted earlier in these pages. The question is, How consistently may the hack be regarded as the narrator? When do we hear his voice and when do we hear Swift's? Given Swift's multifaceted use of irony, the questions are really in the absolute sense unanswerable. Some of us believe, nonetheless, that in many places in the *Tale* volume we are in the presence of Swift himself and in those places it is

Swift's voice that we hear. Section 9, the "Digression Concerning Madness" is one of those places.

What John Traugott calls an often "hopelessly complex" problem is this interesting confusion caused by Swift's irony. So here, in the passages I have just been quoting, Traugott asks, "[I]s it a 'persona' who speaks? is it Swift the Anglican rationalist? is it Swift the diabolist? is it confusion worse confounded? . . . Then the critic, like a traffic policeman, shrilly signals which way to go: *here,* for an instant, Swift shows himself through the mask, or is it *there?* or everywhere? or nowhere?"[32]

Clearly there are various points of view on this matter and various conclusions that these points of view deliver to us. Ronald Paulson, for example, concludes that, if we rightly hear the "voice" of Swift behind the voice of his narrator, we may discover "What Swift is representing in the *Tale* is the general outline of an ideal—the concept of the rounded citizen. . . ."[33] Such a citizen would consider the hack's ideas entirely and outrageously wrong. Irvin Ehrenpreis reaches a position somewhat comparable to Paulson's: "My only postulate is that behind the book [the *Tale*] stands not a list of philosophical propositions but the idea of a good man."[34]

Whatever stance a reader takes regarding the hack (and what he is saying) and Swift (and what he says and means), we are safe enough if we return to Swift's own comment in the "Apology": he intended his emphasis to be on "Abuses in Religion" and "Those in Learning." As my remarks in this chapter indicate, he achieved a very large measure of success in this stated intention. I also believe, however, that when in highly charged moments his imaginative use of myths and symbols carried him inexorably out of his priestly role, he achieved a great deal more than his stated intention. How much more and what more is a mooted question, as my comments and citations have attempted to demonstrate. The "more" I would insist upon. The degree and mature of this "moreness" will always be a challenging problem for each reader to ponder.

After the "Digression concerning Madness" come "A Farther Digression (section 10), the return to the religious allegory in section 11, and the "Conclusion"[35] of the *Tale.* These sections seem distinctly anticlimactic. The prose is occasionally forceful; the expository passages reinforce—and the additional details about Jack—dramatically validate, underlying themes in the great "Digression concerning Madness."

It might be said that, rhetorically speaking, these last sections of the *Tale* wind things down after the tension of the climax in section 9.

A Discourse concerning the Mechanical Operation of the Spirit. In a Letter to a Friend. A Fragment is the third, last, and least highly regarded section of the *Tale* volume. It is a relatively short section—about twenty-five pages in a modern text. Here are modern hack—if we allow him to be the "author" of this section also—seems in his insane ways to be much like the narrator we have become familiar with in the *Battle* and the *Tale*. In this *Fragment* he proposes to treat upon "Religious Enthusiasm, or launching out the soul, as an Effect of Artifice and Mechanic Operation." Enthusiastic preachers, ministers who appeal to their audiences' emotions rather than to their reason, humming and droning through their syphilitic noses, achieve the desired pitch of spirit by mechanistic means. The audience mechanistically induces itself into a trance-like state. The hack's words are: "I conceive the methods of this art to be a point of useful knowledge in a very few hands, and which the learned world would gladly be informed." In fact the entire *Discourse* may be taken as in some ways a parody of some pompous "mechanic's" report to the Royal Academy of Science, a satiric butt that Swift will gleefully assault again in book 3 of *Gulliver's Travels*.

How does the religious dissident mechanistically "launch out his soul" into the trance-like state he longs for? What are his methods? Our narrator, characteristically detailed in his instruction, tells how these religionists go about it. They "violently strain their eyeballs inward, half closing the lids. . . ." The narrator continues after a bit saying, "[A]t first, you can see nothing; but after a short pause a small glimmering light begins to appear, and dance before you. Then by frequently moving your body up and down, you perceive the vapours to ascend very fast, till your are perfectly dosed and flustered, like one who drinks too much in a morning. Meanwhile the preacher is also at work: he begins a loud hum which pierces you quite through; this is immediately returned by the audience, and you find yourself prompted to imitate them, by a mere spontaneous impulse, without knowing what you do."

The narrator cannot long sustain his attempt at an objective posture. We soon hear him scold: "I am resolved immediately to weed this error out of mankind." Then, though dissenting Jack (of the *Tale*) is not named, it is Jack (or any other dissenter) who is attacked: among these people, "cant and droning supply the place of sense and reason." "Hawking, spitting, and belching, the defects of other men's rhetoric, are the flower, and the figures, and ornaments of his." We then get a hardly relevant "history of fanaticism," which includes the ancient and still familiar charge that religious zeal and enthusiasm correlate closely with gross sexuality: "Persons of visionary devotion, either men or women, are, in their complexion, of all others the most amorous."

At its close, the *Mechanical Operation* attempts to retain the fiction, earlier introduced, that it is a letter to a friend: "Pray burn this Letter as soon as it comes to your Hands." The fiction was a conventional one during Swift's era, and we take it too seriously if we say that the device does not here succeed: it hardly ever did. It is quite probable that Swift introduced it merely to spoof its absurdity since, as we know, much of his satire had a literary basis. However, it is of more import to note that in this *Mechanical Operation of the Spirit,* and for the last time in the *Tale* volume, a major theme is struck. *The Mechanical Operation* tells us that "The first ingredient towards the Art of Canting is a competent share of *inward light.*" With this comment we are back in sections 8 and 9 and parts of 11 of the *Tale* itself. A representative and relevant passage appears in section 8, where we are told that "the original cause of all things [is] wind" and that the oracular belch of the wise Aeolist is "the noblest act of a rational creature." Here I think it is Swift himself talking again and thus paradoxically it is this Irish priest who tells us not for a moment to trust the inward light. It is, after all, the product of mere wind—vapors rising from a stinking jakes below. To trust such religious enthusiasm or "light" is madness.

Evaluations

Discerning and knowledgable students of Swift, having read and reread *A Tale of a Tub, The Battle of the Books,* and *The Mechanical Operation of the Spirit,* inevitably say at some point in their lives that this is the best volume that Swift ever wrote. Furthermore, the best part of this best volume is *A Tale of a Tub,* the finest prose satire that Swift ever wrote. Moreover, *The Battle of the Books* is indisputably one of the most outstanding mock-heroic prose works in our language. So the comments go. They are not the comments of the average reader who, if he reads the *Tale* volume at all, will generally compare it to *Gulliver's Travels,* which he has probably already read. Among other criticisms, such readers say that the book sometimes bogs down in merely cerebral wit and unbelievable hyperbole, and that the digressions are overused almost past endurance. As a consequence, for many readers the *Tale* volume has by no means the impact that *Gulliver's Travels* has. Alas, even some learned readers react negatively. Professor Donald Bruce reports, feelingly, "a more quibbling critic might consider that Swift's prose style, with its hedging mysteriousness, its shuffling archly backwards and forwards, its elaborately concessive manner and its facetious circumstances, resembles nothing more than one of those Chinese carvings from a single piece of ivory in which a fretted globe revolves round a fretted globe containing nothing more than a fretted globe. . . . Surely no joke was ever so ponderously and so protractedly wearisome as the diction of *The Tale of a Tub!*"[36]

There are several reasons for the negative comments about the *Tale* volume, and they explain why *Gulliver's Travels* is the more widely read book. One obvious reason is that the Gulliver persona gives a relatively consistent point of view to the *Travels,* a quality lacking in the *Tale* volume. The modern hack of the *Tale* volume is apparently a useful figure to so many readers that I have not hesitated to employ him. But it is clear that as a fictive device he has to be regarded with suspicion. He is not used in a consistent way; he is rarely convincing as a character. The consequence, as Downie has told us, is "mystification." Certainly Gulliver is not used with the entire consistency either, but he is the cause of much less mystification, probably because he seems for the most part a "real" narrator and an interesting character. (Only book 3 of *Gulliver's Travels* presents serious problems.) Also, Swift's control of a narrative line, at its best in *Gulliver's Travels,* is weak in the *Tale* volume. The story as a consequence is hardly one that holds children from play and old men from the chimney corner. In fact, only in the spider and bee episode and in certain sections of the history of Peter, Martin, and Jack is there much story at all.

Readers of the *Tale* volume are also disturbed by the nature of the satire and the frequent ambiguities of the irony. For instance, we can quite reasonably wonder when to stop scoffing at a dissenter's "enthusiasm" or "inward light" (which Swift mercilessly ridicules) and when to begin admiring a judicious admixture of it in a Church of England dean. After all, as Swift wrote some years later in his *Letter to a Young Gentleman* (1720), "If your Arguments be strong, in God's name offer them in as moving a Manner as the Nature of the Subject will properly admit. . . ." Swift does hedge a bit here, but apparently he is not dismissing the value of some degree of enthusiasm. Which Swift are we supposed to believe? And sometimes, too, Swift's satire is rather sprayed than aimed. The consequence is that his ostensibly intended target becomes in effect a whole group of other targets. The brutal satire on the sacraments and the mysteries of Redemption and Incarnation of the Roman Catholic Church is so generalized that it also attacks the many Protestant Churches' sacraments of baptism and the Lord's Supper and their Mysteries. The resultant ambiguities have always been troublesome for readers and of course for Swift himself because, however ardently a man wants to defend his church and its tenets, he cannot win friends in his own Christian church if, while swept along on the wings of an exciting metaphor, he attacks rites shared by almost all Christian churches, including his own. He cannot—purporting merely to be quoting his narrator, but fooling nobody—he cannot attack religion itself, which he actually seems on occasion to be doing, without upsetting a great many readers. His friend, Bishop Atterbury, was quite right when he wrote, "The author of *A Tale of a Tub* will not as yet be known; and if it be the man I guess, he hath reason to conceal himself, because of the prophane strokes in that piece, which would do his reputation and interest in the world more harm than good." Atterbury's attitude was widespread enough to make almost convincing the legend about the lines attached to the door of St. Patrick's Cathedral, on the day Swift was installed there as its dean, in June 1713:

> Look down, St. Patrick, look, we pray
> On Thine own Church and Steeple;
> Convert thy Dean, on this Great Day;
> Or else God help the People![37]

Finally, in comparing the *Tale*-volume with *Gulliver's Travels*, readers would for the most part agree that the *Tale* volume is more witty than humorous and does not yield anything like the amount of delightful and uncomplicated whimsy of the *Travels*. We recall in book 1, when Swift is describing the handwriting of the six-inch-tall Lilliputians, he says that they wrote "aslant from one corner of the paper to the other, like ladies in England." (Is this a tease directed at Stella?) Then there is the account of little Gulliver taking a flying leap over the enormous pile of dung left by a Brobdingnagian cow. Not flying far enough, poor Gulliver lands up to his knees in dung (To say this funny scene suggests that man's pride leads him to attempts that common sense should teach him to shun is an absurdly pretentious piece of explication.) We remember little Gulliver rowing that huge boat in the

Brobdingnagian tub, a boat which Glumdalclitch always carried ("when I had done") ". . . into her closet, and hung . . . on a nail to dry." Thus Gulliver's littleness and insignificance in this land of giants (book 2) is emphasized. In book 4, "The Voyage to the Houyhnhnms," we laugh when, after athletic competition among the young horses ("the youth" of that land), "the victor was rewarded with a song in his or her praise." Horses singing? Come now. The *Tale* volume, because it gives us comparatively little of this sort of simple fun, is proportionately a less engaging book for the average reader, and indeed for most readers, than is *Gulliver's Travels.*

In the end, our task is to look as squarely as we can at the *Tale* volume itself and attempt some sort of assessment. We can say it is a powerful book, a brilliant book, a clever book, a fascinating book, a disturbing book, a confusing and ambiguous book, and so on and on, and there would be some truth in every one of these assessments.

I think the *Tale* volume is a great book. Its greatness lies in such unforgettable passages as the altercation between the spider and the bee in the *Battle,* or in the terrifying story of the bird of paradise in section 8, or in the "Digression concerning Madness" in section 9. These passages tell us that it is important to get to the truth about things. Self-deception is avoidable if "fancy is not astride reason" and "imagination is not at cuff with the senses." If we use our reason we can flay the rind off and see the kernel beneath the rind. In Swift's world the kernel will probably not be very attractive, but at least it will be discovered for what it is. This discovery is good. The famous digression on madness will also allow the conclusion, I believe, that there are humane ways to get at the truth and there are inhumane (inhuman, irrational, and insane) ways. Flaying a woman alive is not a humane way. Swift does not reveal to us what the humane way is. He never does. Some readers will insist that, since the inhumane way is revealed to us by the hack-narrator, and since the hack is mad, Swift, as a sane man, does not and could not possibly agree with him. This may be so. It seems to me a defensible interpretation, though here Mr. Downie's caution is certainly applicable: "we can never be sure."

My personal inclination, however, is to accept Traugott's comment, which echoes a position earlier and more fully developed by Émile Pons. Traugott writes, "Parody [which was Swift's satiric device] led him to a sympathy (perhaps largely unconscious, though not entirely so) with the enemy he mocked, so that in the grubby or mad postures he affects he is liberated from the decorums of his class and office. He can be as libertine as he pleases speaking in the crazy metaphysical conceits and ingenuities of the character parodied."[38]

In these passionate occasions when his imagination is "liberated" Swift went considerably beyond his stated intention of satirizing abuses in religion and learning. If all religious rites are inventions of charlatans, and if, as he seems to say, "reason and logic are but the product and afflux of filthy vapours of the brain,"[39] then what of religion and learning? They do not exist.

This nihilistic conclusion need not be, and is not, shared by all readers, though I am myself partial to the conviction that at this time in a life replete as his was with frustrations and defeats, Swift himself believed it. But let us remember that there are many other ways to read the *Tale* volume. In this book I have touched on only a few and mainly on those that interest me the most. Various as interpretations are, however, I believe most readers would agree that, as powerfully as anybody in our literature, Swift enunciated the need to crack the shells and find the kernels. No one ever more effectively depicted the terrible dangers that must ensue if we ignore this teaching and allow imagination to get astride our reason and let sense yield the reins to fancy. No doubt many reasonable men and women are grateful to Swift, even if grudgingly, for making this harsh warning unforgettable.

Perhaps our respect for the man and his book should restrain the easy comment that elsewhere in his writing there are elements that belie the dourly one-sided implications of the *Tale* volume. I cite only the scores and scores of delightful letters and verses to and from his friends, verses rich in "fancy" and "imagination." No doubt about it. But none of this evidence changes anything. The confusions in this volume remain; the tasteless and labored puerilities remain; the brilliance and the incredible flights of imagination remain; the passions remain.

Whatever passionate conclusions his liberated imagination led him to, Swift (so frequently paradoxical) also gave his allegiance to the importance of reason. As a product of the Age of Reason, he endorsed the concept that reason would prevail, if we but let it; that reason ought to prevail, and we should let it. Fancy is therefore to be excoriated; undisciplined imagination is excommunicated and reason alone is idealized. Some readers find this another one of the unsatisfactory and uncomfortable theses propounded by the *Tale* volume. I doubt, however, that any serious reader has ever thought that this thesis did not need to be stated, that it should not have been stated, and that it is not a good thing that it has been stated. Nobody should therefore take lightly this strange, disturbing, but so often captivating book. Swift told us that he would expose abuses in religion and learning, and he did. But in those exciting moments when his imagination liberated him from his priestly role, he told us quite a lot more, too, and asked us to ponder their unsettling implications. To have achieved so much is a sufficient accomplishment.

Chapter Three
Later Prose of the English Years

Propagandist and Pamphleteer

In 1712 Swift was forty-five years old. He had to his credit a small clutch of good poems; he was known as the author of *A Tale of a Tub;* he had written, or was about to write, a number of prose works of great and immediate importance; and he was in England. When the Tories came to power in 1710, "their great difficulty," he wrote in 1714 in his *Memoirs, Relating to That Change in the Queen's Ministry in 1710,* "lay in the Want of some good Pen to keep up the Spirit raised in the People, to assert the Principles, and justify the Proceedings of the new Ministers. . . ."

Swift became the "good pen" that the ministry needed. As the chief journalist for and historian of the Tory party during Queen Anne's reign, he was impressively successful. As editor of the *Examiner,* he did great good for his party; in his *Conduct of the Allies* he wrote one of the most successful pieces of party propaganda in journalistic history. He also worked very hard and long on his *History of the Four Last Years of the Queen*—a book intended to vindicate a Tory ministry for which he had given so much of himself; and from which, at the end, he got so very much less than he had hoped for. His *History* was not published during his lifetime.

Much of Swift's prose is read today only by specialists. Some of the prose, like *The Four Last Years,* is read only by very dedicated specialists, since it has slight value as literature. Many of the essays in the *Examiner* are rarely read these days because, I suppose, they deal with personalities and political issues quite foreign to most of us. But it should be insisted that this is not always so. The *Examiner* of 9 November 1710, "An Essay upon the Art of Political Lying," is timely, anytime. In the essay of 4 January 1710 Swift writes with dry irony of the Whig protectors of the church: "To shew their zeal for the church's defence, they took the care of it entirely out of the hands of God almighty (because that was a foreign jurisdiction) and made it their own creature." "Though," as Swift said in another fine essay in this collection, "I am an Examiner only, and not a Reformer" (8 February 1710), a fuller discussion of his thirty-three essays contributed to the *Examiner* would demonstrate the truth of the Ehrenpreis conclusion: "Through all the numbers, Swift had one obvious, repeated theme— the superiority of the Tories to the Whigs."[1] He did of course examine; but he most certainly hoped also to reform.

On 27 November 1711 was published another prose work that, like a number of the essays in the *Examiner,* deserves to be read more often than it is. It was a pamphlet entitled *The Conduct of the Allies.* The Tory ministry could of course by expected to encourage its sale, for its intent was to justify the treaty that the ministry had devised to end the war with France. Party leaders—and the printer—must nonetheless have been delighted that the publication did so well: within little more than a month an astronomical (for those days) eleven thousand copies were sold.[2]

The situation that brought forth this famous pamphlet may be briefly summarized. In 1701 England joined with its allies—the Netherlands and Austria—to form the so-called Grand Alliance to prevent France and Spain from being joined under one king and thus establishing a naval, colonial, and economic superpower that they correctly regarded as a threat to their interests. The resultant War of the Spanish Succession was prosecuted vigorously by the Whig administration then in power in England and progressed generally in favor of England and its allies, in large part because of the brilliant generalship of England's duke of Marlborough (a Whig) and of Prince Eugene of Austria. Not long after Harley and Bolingbroke and their Tory party came into power in 1710, however, England engaged France in secret unilateral negotiations to end the hostilities. When the details of these negotiations became known, the Whig opposition was predictably furious. The English seemed to them to have deserted—even betrayed—their allies by unilaterally and covertly coming to terms with their common enemy.

"There is now but one business the ministry wants me for," Swift wrote in his *Journal to Stella* (25 August 1711). The "business" was the defense of the new treaty, and it was accomplished in *The Conduct of the Allies.*

The performance was a remarkable one on all counts. Its author first carefully established, as his "voice," a persona that ranks among his most successful. The persona begins by telling us that he "thinks it highly necessary that the publick should be freely and impartially told what circumstances they are in, after what manner they have been treated by those, whom they trusted so many years with their blood and treasure . . ." (Preface). Then this self-designated impartial narrator speaks of the enormous costs of the war ("If the war be to last another campaign, it will be impossible to find funds for supplying it . . ."); in one way or another he refers again and again to "the monied men" who are "so fond of war" because of course they are making huge profits from it and thus "we have been fighting for the ruin of the publick interest, and the advancement of a private." Next he documents the fact that the allies' conduct has been reprehensible: the Dutch have not helped ("they never once furnished their quota either of ships or men"); the Austrians were no better (they were "by stipulation to furnish ninety thousand men against the common enemy," but the quota was met only once during the whole war). In short, all the evidence given by this thoughtful and sober narrator reveals that England's allies in the war had not done their part and had taken shameful advantage of an England that was going bankrupt in its efforts to satisfy the greed of "the monied men," including even the great duke of Marlborough. (In one of his *Examiner* essays [23 November 1710] Swift had given some of the details about the huge profits that Marlborough had made.) Now, as the narrator had said in his preface, "Supposing the war to have commenced upon a just motive; the next thing to be considered is, when a prince ought in prudence to receive the overtures of a peace." The time for such overtures had indisputably arrived. Happily, from Swift's and the ministry's point of view, Parliament was induced after a time to agree.

The Peace of Utrecht was signed in 1713. The war was over. Moreover, on balance, England profited handsomely: for example, it acquired Gibraltar, Hudson's Bay, and Nova Scotia and thus added considerably to its naval and commercial powers. It is not surprising, therefore, that the great historian G. M. Trevelyan has remarked that Swift did more in *The Conduct of the Allies* "to settle the immediate fate of parties and of nations than did ever any other literary man in the annals of England."[3]

Part of the fascination of *The Conduct of the Allies* is that, strangely for Swift, the work is almost entirely lacking in irony. But also of interest is the fact that this objective-seeming pamphlet, "documented" so convincingly, is in fact consistently biased and on occasion downright inaccurate in its record of what purports to be the truth. Did Swift know he was lying? Yes. Only consider his denunciation in *Gulliver's Travels* (3:8) of "the prostitute Writers" of "modern History." But in Works like *The Conduct of the Allies* it is unlikely that he would feel any guilt. Absolute consistency was never Swift's strong point. Besides, he was inordinately proud of his association with great men like Harley and Bolingbroke; he admired them both, moreover, and was of course loyal to their cause. Having been charged with producing a document that would help his friends, his party, and his country out of a war that he had come to think a bad one, he carried out his function superbly. *The Conduct of the Allies* is a memorable example of successful journalistic propaganda.

Two other prose works of these English years deserve mention: one is that delightful, though puzzling, source-document called *The Journal to Stella;* the other is *A Proposal for Correcting, Improving and Ascertaining* [establishing, or "fixing"] *the English Tongue* (1712).

With respect to the *Proposal* two assertions are current: the first is that this pamphlet is one of the very rare publications that appeared under Swift's name; the second, that Swift was wrong in his major thesis. Both generalizations are correct. The "proposal" was in essence that the ministry should establish an English Society equivalent to the French Academy and that this English Society be empowered to halt further corruption of the language by permanently "fixing" its parts: "what I have most at Heart," he wrote, "is, that some Method should be thought on for Ascertaining and Fixing our Language for ever, after such Alterations are made in it as shall be thought requisite. For I am of the Opinion, that it is better a Language should not be wholly perfect, than that it should be perpetually changing: and we must give over at one Time or other, or at length infallibly change for the worse." Swift does slightly qualify his position: he does "not mean that [our language] should never be enlarged: Provided, that no Word, which a Society shall give a Sanction to, be afterwards antiquated and exploded, they may have Liberty to receive whatever new ones they shall find Occasion for." Old books will therefore be forever valued for their intrinsic worth: they can always be read, for their words will always be with us.

Swift's antagonist, Richard Bentley, surely pedant that Swift thought him to be, had nonetheless a clearer understanding of the way language behaves. In his *Dissertation upon Phalaris,* Bentley had written: "Every living language, like the perspiring bodies of living creatures, is in perpetual motion and alteration; some words go off, and become obsolete; others are taken in, and by degrees grow into common use; or the same word is inverted to a new sense and notion, which in . . . time makes as observable a change in the air and features of a language, as age makes in the lines and mien of a face."[4]

Modern linguistic theory is properly impatient with Swift since evidence so overwhelmingly proves that Bentley was right. It is not possible, or even desirable, to halt change in a living language, though it might be possible for people of taste, by their example, to exercise some control over the nature and the rate of change. Perhaps this would have satisfied Swift. In the "Apology" to his *Tale of a Tub* his irony cannot conceal the unexpressed hope: his *Tale,* he wrote, "seems calculated to live at least as long as language and taste admit to no great alterations."

But Swift's untenable position in this really masterly written essay is perfectly consistent with his stand on other matters: he did not like change; he liked reason, order, and wise authority. Since opposition to change in language merely meant, to him, an opposition to corruption in language, his position is entirely understandable. He was a writer and a lover of literature, and so were many of his closest friends. We should therefore expect that he would be attracted to what Professor Landa calls "a sanctioned standard language, in order to give permanent life to all written records"—including his own.

The Journal to Stella

Among the most interesting of Swift's writings during this time was a group of letters that he wrote to his two spinster friends now living in Ireland, Esther Johnson (Stella) and Mrs. Dingley. Though the letters were never addressed solely to Stella, they are grouped under the title *The Journal to Stella* and have been so grouped and so titled since Thomas Sheridan first assembled and published them in the latter part of the eighteenth century.[6]

Swift wrote his first *Journal* entry on 1 September 1710 in Chester, just after he landed in England. His last letter was written in Chester on 6 June 1713 just before he left England to spend his next thirty-five years as Dean of St. Patrick's Cathedral in Dublin. The sixty-five letters in the *Journal* are an invaluable social and political document, aside from their considerable biographical worth. They often read like bulletins that an affectionate cousin or uncle, away on business, might send home to his family. Swift wrote nothing else quite like them. (He was forty-three in 1710; Stella was twenty-nine, and Swift had known her since she was about eight. Rebecca Dingley was about forty-four.) Except for a time after 1711—when Swift was ill, terribly busy, or worried about the fate of the Tory ministry—the tone of the letters is usually warm.[7]

Swift employed a kind of "family language," using invented terms like "Presto" (Swift) and "MD" (My Dear on My Dears); he is marvellously conversational—as good letter writers generally are; and he presents many details about himself. The letters are also full, but not too full, of details about his work. For example, he proudly tells how he moves among the great ones of his day: "Mr. Harley came out to me, brought me in, and presented me to his son-in-law, Lord Doblane (or some such name) and his own son, and, among others, Will Penn the quaker: we sat two hours drinking as good wine as you do; and two hours more he and I alone" (30 September 1710).[8]

Although he writes about his work, he is usually, and perhaps deliberately, vague as to details. The last line of the passage just quoted illustrates this. Here are some others:

I design to stay here all the next week, to be at leisure by myself, to finish something of weight I have upon my hands. . . . (29 September 1711)

I was this afternoon in the city, eat a bit of meat, and settled some things with a printer. (18 October 1711)

I have had a Visitor here that has taken up my time. (21 March 1713)

The rhetorical problem Swift faced in the situations referred to in these excerpts was not only to guard against giving away state secrets to spies who intercepted the mails but also, negatively stated, simply to avoid freighting his account with a too heavy load of details about his job. Too much information about routine daily chores would make documentaries out of familiar letters. The special pitch to which Swift tuned for these letters would hardly admit very much of the thick sound of factuality. And that he did intend a special tone is indicated by an entry like this one of 10 May 1712: "I have not yet ease or Humor enough to go on in my Journal Method." The tone itself is sounded in such lines as ". . . methinks you were here and I were prating to you" (16 January 1711).

Indeed, much of the *Journal* has the tone of a friendly, family-type chat. A reader seems actually to hear the writer conversing avuncularly, as though his two dear spinster friends were right there with him:

Faith, this is a whole treatise; I'll go reckon the lines on t'other side. I've reckoned them.

(12 October 1710)

And so get you gone to ombre [a card game], and be good girls, and save your money, and be rich against Presto [Swift] comes, and write to me now and then: I am thinking it would be a pretty thing to hear sometimes from sawcy MD; but don't hurt your eyes, Stella,[9] I charge you [12 October 1710]. . . . [I] am now got into bed . . . to open your letter; and God send I may find MD well, and happy, and merry, and that they love Presto as they do fires. Oh, I won't open it yet! yes I will! no I won't; . . . . What shall I do? My fingers itch; and I now have it in my left hand; and now I'll open it this very moment. . . . Pshaw, 'tis from Sir Andrew Fountain. . . .

(14 October, 1710)

In other samplings from *The Journal* Swift talks about writing that he has done or is doing, including a reference to a poem he had written: "This day came out the *Tatler* made up wholly of my *Shower* [the poem], and a preface to it. They say 'tis the best thing I ever writ, and I think so too" (17 October 1710). Or: I have been 6 hours to day morning writing 19 pages of a Lettr to day to Ld Treasr, about forming a Society or Academy to correct and fix the English Language" (21 February 1712). He grumbles about his manservant, the immortal Patrick: "I have a mind to turn that puppy away: he has been drunk ten times in three weeks. But I han't time to say more; so good night, etc." (18 October 1710). He speaks often of his health, or lack of it: "I have left off lady Kerry's bitter, and got another box of pills. I have no fits of giddiness, but only some little disorder towards it; and I walk as much as I can" (13 February 1711).

He also writes of his hopes for a clerical appointment:

This morning My Friend Mr. Lewis came to me, and shewed me an Order for a Warrant for the 3 vacant Deanryes, but none of them to me; this was what I always foresaw, and receive the notice of it better I believe than he expected. . . . [A]t Noon Ld Tr hearing, I was in Mr. Lewis's office, came to me

& sd many things too long to repeat. I told him I had nothing to do but go to Ireld immediately, for I could not with any Reputation stay longer here, unless I had something honorable immediately given to me.

(13 April 1713)

And he gossips: "Odso, I forgot; . . . . Mrs. Tisdal is very big, ready to ly down. Her Husband is a puppy" (6 June 1713).

What Swift does not do is tell his female correspondents the story of his rapidly developing intimacy with the Vanhomrigh family, and particularly with a daughter of this family, Esther, whom Swift called "Hessy" or "Misheskinage" or "Governor Huff" or—his best-known nickname for her—"Vanessa." He seems to have tried to establish with her the same sort of safely platonic relationship he had with Stella. He failed. The relationship probably remained platonic, but it was a stormy affair that brought no credit on him and caused great unhappiness to poor Esther.

Irvin Ehrenpreis some years ago and David Nokes more recently have pointed out the discrepancies between what Swift told Hetty Johnson (Stella) about Hessy Vanhomrigh and what Swift's own account books show to be the facts.[10] Two examples demonstrate the pattern of deception. Swift writes to Stella that "I dined privately with a friend to-day in the neighbourhood" (13 November 1711); the account book spells it out: "Wine. Van's 1s.6d." (Accounts 1711–12, fol. 3). Again, in another entry he speaks of dining with "a friend in St. James's-street" (19 November 1711), but his accounts quite specifically reveal that he had on this occasion played piquet at Mrs. Vanhomrigh's and probably had dinner there also (Accounts 1711–12, fol. 1). Swift was quite obviously not telling Stella anything like the whole truth. Despite this discomforting information about his devious behavior, however, the revelations by no means detract from our interest in, and our respect for, this very unusual book.

Writing about the letters to Stella and Dingley, William Irving concludes perceptively by referring to "the strange picture they leave of Swift as delightful friend, moralist, schoolmaster, and damned soul. . . . The pain of things is there and elsewhere in Swift's letters and gives his whole production a peculiarly Vergilian power over the imagination, till men say that these must be among the great letters of all time."[11] Such very high praise does not in this instance seem unreasonable.

"The Conclusion, in Which Nothing Is Concluded"

During these few English years Swift wrote a tremendous amount of prose, much of it narrowly topical. Perhaps it should therefore be recalled how very selective this chapter is: attention has been directed to those writings that have transcended the occasions that produced them. With such an aim in mind, *The Journal to Stella*, essays from the *Examiner*, *The Conduct of the Allies*, and *The Proposal for Correcting, Improving and Ascertaining the English Tongue* have seemed to me the prose most immediately appropriate to this study, and for that reason deserved to be looked at in some detail.

Only one other problem should be noted: this problem is that *The Journal to Stella* just as inevitably raises, as does any discussion of the poetry of Swift, the question of his relationship with the two young women, mentioned in this document, whose friendship he cultivated: Stella and Vanessa. Of these two, Stella was far and away the more important, for it must be admitted that finally, as Ehrenpreis states, Vanessa was only "a peripheral pastime, a quasi-mistress."[12] And it is about Stella, in any case, that the *Journal* more insistently raises questions. Harold Williams remarks that the "enigmatic relationship" between her and Swift, "a relationship which continued without change on either hand, for thirty years or more, has puzzled every inquirer."[13] No doubt all Swift scholars hope that the truth will someday be known, even if every passing year makes that prospect less likely. One of Swift's earliest biographers, John Hawkesworth, concluded that Swift and Stella were married. But Hawkesworth adds, ". . . Why [this] marriage was so cautiously concealed, and why he was never known to meet her but in the presence of a third person, are enquiries which no man can answer, without absurdity, and are therefore unprofitable objects of speculation."[14] I do not believe that the force of the last part of Hawkesworth's comment has as yet been sufficiently felt. If it is ever felt, or if the truth is ever known, one obviously tangential but happily immediate benefit will be a cessation of speculation about the problem. Another will perhaps be that some scholars who have heretofore addressed themselves with tremendous cleverness and zeal to the puzzle will turn their fine intelligences to a study of other scholarly and critical problems about which more facts are available and answers more urgently needed.[15] Meanwhile, I believe that the conclusion must be like Samuel Johnson's in *Rasselas*, "a conclusion, in which nothing is concluded." However, the reader who wishes to pursue this particular question might be advised to begin by consulting Maxwell B. Gold's *Swift's Marriage to Stella.* Though committed to a thesis (Swift and Stella were married), Gold's systematic assembling of the known evidence is still a useful introduction. Another convenient source is David Nokes's *Jonathan Swift,* wherein can be found a paragraph that handily summarizes the responses of some of our major biographers to this problem: Sheridan and Hawkesworth thought that Swift and Stella were married; Ehrenpries "evades the issue"; Downie believes there is "conclusive evidence against the marriage"; Nokes considers that "the balance of probabilities . . . favours the notion of the secret marriage."[16] I do not myself think that there was a marriage. Thus the major truth at this point seems to be that there is, alas, no consensus on this question and nothing can be concluded.

Chapter Four
The Left-handed Poet

In middle age, Swift referred to himself as one who "had the Sin of Wit no venial Crime; / Nay, 'twas affirm'd, he sometimes dealt in Rhime: / Humour, and Mirth, had Place in all he writ" ("The Author Upon Himself" [1714]). If Swift was not quite accurate, "Humour and Mirth" do inform a great deal, if not all, of his poetry; and in his comment that he "sometimes dealt in Rhime," he is guilty only of hugely understating the facts. Though to my knowledge no one has counted lines to prove this point, it is probably safe to say that of significant Augustan Age poets only Swift's friend Alexander Pope wrote more poetry than he did. (Harold Williams did not count the number of lines, but he reports that Swift wrote "two hundred and fifty genuine poems,"[1] in addition to a considerable number of riddles and epigrams in verse.) Also, Pope generally wrote better poetry and was more careful of his literary estate; much of Swift's poetry moved rather accidentally into the public domain.

Interest in Swift's poetry has increased substantially during the past three or four decades and some extremely valuable studies bear witness to this fact. For example, during one five-year period, 1977–81, five major books appeared as well as numerous critical and scholarly articles.[2] This is not to say that Swift's poetry has finally been rediscovered in our time. If critics have not often over the years treated the poetry fully or always fairly, it has never been really ignored. In Swift's own century, Deane Swift, son of one of his cousins, and Samuel Johnson spoke seriously about it; so did Sir Walter Scott and the wise Sir Henry Craik, in the nineteenth century; and in this century, scholars such as Sir Harold Williams (*The Poems of Jonathan Swift*, 1937), Maurice Johnson (*The Sin of Wit*, 1950), and Joseph Horrell (*Collected Poems of Jonathan Swift*, 1958), have ensured that interest in Swift's poetry would be kept very much alive. The impressive number of recent studies is a most welcome addition, however, to these earlier ones.

Few of the critics of any period give much attention to Swift's first poems. The reasons can perhaps be suggested by a look at his first work, the "Ode to the Athenian Society" (published in 1692, when

Swift was twenty-five years old). In this ode we find lines of such irremediable flatness as "No sooner does she land / On the delightful Strand / When strait she sees the Country all around" (ll. 36–38). We also confront a nearly unbelievable (for Swift) rhetorical posture reflected in these lines: "But as for poor contented me, / Who must my weakness and my ignorance confess . . ." (ll. 132–33).

The occasional doggerel, the bathos, and the false posturing of this and other odes published during these early years have probably prompted some readers to hope that these early poems had not survived. This attitude is unfortunate in a way, for the early poems have undeniable interest as revealing autobiographical documents;[3] they do interestingly shadow forth themes and metaphors of major import in the later works; and they really are, as Professor Quintana with seraphic charity remarks about Swift's Pindaric odes, "by no means the worst of their kind."[4] Such observations are not intended to make good poems out of mediocre ones,[5] however.

Though Swift started out seriously enough to be a poet,[6] he began— as is the fashion sometimes with young writers—by imitating authors he admired: Abraham Cowley ("when I writt what pleases me I am Cowley to my self," said Swift[7]) and his patron, Sir William Temple ("I prefer him to all others at present in England"[8]). Abraham Cowley (1618–67) was highly and widely esteemed, particularly for his Pindaric odes. Samuel Johnson's sardonic comment was that "All the boys and girls caught the pleasing fancy, and they could do nothing else but write like Pindar."[9] Since neither Pindar's nor Cowley's nor Temple's gait, so to say, was Swift's, his attempts to emulate these mentors were predictably disappointing.

However, despite the adverse criticism by Quintana—and also by Pons, who called it "simply an exercize in monumental bad taste"[10]— the "Ode to the Athenian Society" does raise one of our more intriguing biographical questions, for it is still widely believed to have inspired this comment from John Dryden: "Cousin Swift, you will never be a poet." Johnson's source for this anecdote is not known. An earlier and more credible, though less crisply quotable, version appeared in Colley Cibber's *Lives of the Poets* (1753); in it Dryden is reported to have remarked, "Cousin Swift, turn your thoughts some other way, for nature has never formed you for a Pindaric poet." Because Cibber is vague about the source of his information, this story may be merely another of the many fables that have stubbornly barnacled themselves to biographies of Swift.[11] At any rate, if it was not Dryden, who or what did cause young Swift to stop, to pause, and then to start his poetry off on a different and more successful track? Nobody knows. However, in probably the best of these much derided early poems, a work entitled "Occasioned by Sir W[illiam] T[emple]'s Late Illness and Recovery" (1693), we do learn when and to some extent why the change occurred. Though in this work Sir William and his illness are alluded to, the real subject matter is quite something else. Instead of celebrating his happiness that all the dangers of the "late illness" have passed, Swift turned his attention to Swift: to an exposition of his own private laments, the consequence of his listening to his Muse—that "wild form dependent on the brain / . . . a glitt'ring voice, a painted name, / A walking vapor . . ." (ll. 95, 101–2). I take it that the "walking vapor" refers to all those illusions we cherish and shall be asked again and again to think about in Swift's later works.

The poet continues: "[T]o be poetically great," he had tried to follow the muse's rule, and as he talks we again hear the voice we shall grow more and more to recognize. The rules:

> Stoop not to intr'est, flattery, or deceit;
> Learn to disdain their mercenary aid;
> Be this thy sure defence, thy brazen wall,
> Know no base action, at no guilt turn pale. . . .
> (ll. 139–42)

Trying to follow the rules of the "Malignant goddess" (l. 81), his muse, Swift's only reward was to be left an "abandoned wretch" (l. 108). Therefore he concluded with this decision: "I here renounce thy visionary pow'r / And since thy essence on my breath depends, / Thus with a puff the whole delusion ends" (ll. 152–54).

"Occasioned by Sir W——T——'s Late Illness and Recovery" obviously does not fulfill the promise indicated by its title, for it does not say much about Temple's illness; but it is nonetheless an instructive poem on at least a couple of levels. It shows Swift deserting once more the Pindaric form, as he already had earlier, in his "To Mr. Congreve." This time he has abandoned it forever. But what most strongly informs the poem is, I believe, Swift's sense of frustration with his career, with (I have supposed) the continued subservience of his position at Moor Park, and with all the terrible humiliations subservience forced upon his abnormally testy and touchy pride. In such circumstances it was not unexpected that he felt "Forsook by hopes, ill fortune's last relief" (l.

109). I believe there was real and continual pain and perhaps even anger for these reasons rather than merely for his decision to renounce a muse that belonged more to Temple and to Cowley than it ever had to him. I think he may even have concluded that he could endure his loss about as easily, in fact, as had Huck Finn when he renounced persimmons: he did not like them anyway. Of course on this matter I do no more than speculate and there are, no doubt, other possibilities that might be considered. For example, it may be that Swift one day simply decided he would return to the predominantly satiric style native to his earlier days, more natural to him, and so much to his liking that he had once memorized all of Samuel Butler's *Hudibras*, the famous satire on the Puritans. And Herbert Davis refers to the fact that, in his undergraduate commonplace book, Swift had copied out verses that clearly indicated a taste for "satire and buffoonery and occasional poems concerned with public affairs." Such activity truly reflects what Professor Davis calls "an early indication of Swift's natural bent."[12]

The "natural bent" gets its best poetic expression in Swift's later poetry, which is also his most interesting poetic work and the most deserving of study; in the best of it Swift deserves a more generous measure of credit than has sometimes been given him. This comment will, I hope, be justified by comments in the pages that follow, though some of his most impressive poems—like, for example, "The Verses Wrote in a Lady's Ivory Table-Book" and "On Poetry: A Rapsody" [*sic*]—must for reasons of space be here omitted.

The poetry that is regarded as characteristically "Swiftean" began to appear, Ricardo Quintana suggests, about 1698, when the poet "was no longer an immature writer." From this time on he "composed . . . verse of a kind which answered in its fashion to [his] satiric idiom. . . ."[13] In fact, as we know, most of Swift's poetry, satiric and otherwise, was written much later than 1698. Joseph Horrell reminds us that Swift "reached his fiftieth birthday having written only one-fifth the poetry he was to write."[14] It is to some of these later poems that we now direct our attention.

"A Description of a City Shower"

> Careful Observers may fortel the Hour
> (By sure Prognosticks) when to dread a Show'r:
> While Rain depends, the pensive Cat gives o'er

Her Frolicks, and pursues her tail no more.
Returning Home at Night, you'll find the Sink
Strike your offended Sense with double Stink.
If you be wise, then go not far to Dine,
You'll spend in Coach-hire more than save in
                              Wine.
A coming Show'r your shooting Corns presage,
Old aches [two syllables!] throb, your hollow Tooth will rage.
Sauntring in Coffee-house is Dulman seen;
He damns the Climate, and complains of Spleen.
Mean while the South rising with dabbled Wings
A Sable Cloud a-thwart the Welkin flings,
That swill'd more Liquor than it could contain,
And like a Drunkard gives it up again.
Brisk Susan whips her Linen from the Rope,
While the first drizzling Show'r is born aslope,
Such is the Sprinkling which some careless Quean
Flirts on you from her Mop, but not so clean.
You fly, invoke the Gods; then turning, stop
To rail; she singing, still whirls on her Mop.
Not yet, the Dust had shun'd th' unequal Strife,
But aided by the Wind, fought still for Life;
And wafted with its Foe by violent Gust,
'Twas doubtful which was Rain, and which was
                              Dust.
Ah! where must needy Poet seek for Aid,
When Dust and Rain at once his Coat invade;
His Only Coat, where Dust confus'd with Rain,
Roughen the Nap, and leave a mingled Stain.
.   .   .   .
Now from all Parts the swelling Kennels
                              [gutters] flow,
And bear their Trophies with them as they go:
Filth of all Hues and Odours seem to tell
What Street they sail'd from, by their Sight and
                              Smell.
They, as each Torrent drives, with rapid Force
From Smithfield, or St. Pulchre's shape their
                              Course,
And in huge Confluent join at Snow-Hill Ridge,
Fall from the Conduit prone to Holborn-Bridge.
Sweepings from Butchers Stalls, Dung, Guts, and
                              Blood,

> Drown'd Puppies, Stinking Sprats, all drench'd
> in Mud,
> Dead Cats and Turnip-Tops come tumbling down the
> Flood.
>
> (1710)

The numerous references in the *Journal to Stella* tell us how pleased Swift and his readers were with this poem ("They say 'tis the best thing I ever writ, and I think so too"[15] This skillfully constructed poem deserves to be carefully approached and thoughtfully read. It was published on 17 October 1710 in Richard Steele's thrice-weekly *Tatler*, an early version of what we would today call a newspaper. Concerning the poem, we hardly need the reminder, first, that the *Tatler* was not read by shopgirls and blue-collar workers riding home on the subways. Literate people in the coffeehouses (or anywhere else) of those days brought to their reading certain expectations that Swift could depend on (and sometimes did—and sometimes flouted). One of these expectations which he did seem generally to depend on was that his readers would have, or would pretend to have, some knowledge of classical literature. Thus in the description of the storm in this poem they would probably recognize allusions to Virgil's first *Georgic* and to the *Aeneid* ("Troy chairman," "the wooden steed," etc.). Second, we should note the defeat of certain other expectations, most notably that poems were supposed to be written in a flowery, "poetic" diction. Swift's language is often emphatically and in some poems vulgarly antipoetic. In "A City Shower" we see him parodying both the vocabulary and the metaphors of "polite" writing (like "the South rising with Dabbled Wings") with "A Sable Cloud a-thwart the Welkin flings / That swill'd more Liquor than it could contain / And like a Drunkard gives it up again." Or better yet, we should note the "Drown'd Puppies," "stinking Sprats," "Dead Cats," and "Turnip-Tops" of the last stanza. "Here," Swift seems to be saying, "if we must describe a City Shower, let us describe it *as it really is.*" Third, the lines are held tight by the frequent alliteration, of which Swift was fond ("Strike your offended Sense with double Stink"), and with the characteristically abundant internal rhyme and assonance ("While Rain depends, the pensive Cat gives o'er"; "Old Aches throb, your hollow Tooth will rage"). Fourth, we should consider the rhythm and the end-rhymes. To be sure, the last three lines are a triplet (*Blood–Mud–Flood*) concluding with an Alexandrine (a six-stress line). But elsewhere in the poem we hear the familiar heroic couplet of this Augustan age: the rhymes are doublets aa / bb / cc / dd/, etc., and the prevailing rhythm gives us five stresses per line (iambic pentameter). Most of Swift's best-known poems are written in a four-beat line of eight syllables (iambic tetrameter). But in other important respects this poem is characteristic of his best poetry.

I believe that "A City Shower" earns higher marks than Ehrenpreis's grudging "The *Shower* is very good for Swift; it is negligible when set beside many of Pope's and several of Gay's pictures of London."[16] No doubt not as good as some of Pope's and Gay's works; but hardly negligible. Roger Savage argues that "A City Shower" demonstrates "the ludicrous attempt of an imperfect, trivial London to live up to classical dialects and situations."[17] Patricia Spacks and Brendan O Hehir arrive at other judgments. Spacks: the concluding lines of the poem "provide a more forceful indictment of the disorder and filth of the city than could be achieved by ten times their bulk in moral or sociological comment."[18] O Hehir: "The poem's import seems then to lie within its own terms, and to be primarily an oblique denunciation of cathartic doom upon the corruption of the city."[19] Well, maybe so, but it is likely that Swift would be surprised to hear such talk. I believe that more relevant comments should refer to the temperamental and literary basis of the satire in this poem. For, always an antiromantic, Swift would insist that the unpleasant facts about a shower should not be glossed over. We should see it as it is, and that means (Swift always assumes) to see it as he sees it. Also, Swift's satire very often had a literary basis, as it has here. What he ridicules is the unreal language, the affectations, the elegant absurdities of "fashionable," "polite" poetry. He preferred, instead, lines that tell of "Dead Cats and Turnip-Tops [that] come tumbling down the Flood." The same sort of preference is revealed in 1718, with "My master is a parsonable man, and not a spindle-shank'd hoddy-doddy" (from "Mary the Cook-Maid's Letter to Dr. Sheridan"); and again in 1733, for example, "Sit still, and swallow down your spittle" ("On Poetry: A Rapsody").

Poems to Stella

Another of Swift's poems good to look at is "Stella's Birth-day":

> All Travellers at first incline
> Where'er they see the fairest Sign,
> And if they find the Chambers neat,

And like the Liquor and the Meat
Will call again and recommend
The Angel-Inn to ev'ry Friend:
And though the Painting grows decayd
The House will never loose it's Trade;

. . . .

Now, this is Stella's Case in Fact:
An Angel's Face, a little crack't;
(Could Poets or could Painters fix
How Angels look at thirty six)
This drew us in at first to find
In such a Form an Angel's Mind

. . . .

Then Cloe, still go on to prate
Of thirty six, and thirty eight;
Pursue thy Trade of Scandall picking,
Thy Hints that Stella is no Chickin,
Your Innuendo's when you tell us
That Stella loves to talk with Fellows
But let me warn thee to believe
A Truth for which thy Soul should grieve,
That, should you live to see the Day
When Stella's Locks must be grey
When Age must print a furrow'd Trace
On ev'ry Feature of her Face;
Though you and all your senceless Tribe
Could Art or Time or Nature bribe
To make you look like Beauty's Queen
And hold for ever at fifteen.
No Bloom of Youth can ever blind
The Cracks and Wrinckles of your Mind,
All Men of Sense will pass your Dore
And crowd to Stella's at fourscore.

(1721)

Swift wrote eleven poems to Stella, and seven of these were birth-day poems. The birthday present given to her in 1721—selections from this poem are reprinted above—is one of the most engaging of them all. It exhibits many of Swift's characteristic poetic devices: the four-stress line; the *aa* / *bb* / *cc* rhyme scheme; the frequent alliteration and assonance; the diction almost always at "middle level" and as studiously unelevated as the author could make it; the marvelous ability (Pope had it, too) to confine to the couplet-form both the sense and the intonation of ordinary talk. This birthday poem to Stella also reveals familiar Swiftean touchstones like the preeminent importance of mind and the necessity for getting beneath the mere appearance of things. The poem is characterized, finally, by the teasing but beautiful tenderness in Swift's attitude toward this remarkable woman. She transcribed for publication many of Swift's poems, and I cannot think that in this instance she found the chore a dull one. Besides, she was not thirty-six, or even thirty-eight, as the poem states; she was all of forty and must have been grateful for Swift's customary carelessness with dates.

As with *The Journal to Stella,* a by no means incidental point is the "evidence" that this and other birthday poems add to the much-mooted question of the Swift-Stella marriage. The "evidence" is obviously subjective. Nonetheless, there is certainly some truth in Quintana's remark that, "if there is anywhere a key to the enigmatic relations between Swift and Stella, it lies in these extraordinary occasional pieces."[20] Unfortunately, the way this "key" is used is likely to reveal more about the critic himself than about Swift and Stella. Nonetheless, I must risk my conviction that the poems to Stella ("no Chickin" she), none of which say anything about marriage, suggest again that Swift never crossed, with her, the thin line, miles wide, between tenderness and ardor. He loved Stella, but not *that* way. A fondly teasing tone is by no means inimical (in fact, may contribute?) to a romantic attachment; but the attachment cannot be based on this tone alone. There has to be something more. Such lines as, "And though the Painting grows decayd / The House will never loose it's Trade" and "Now this is Stella's Case in Fact: / An Angel's Face, a little crack't" reveal a teasing and affectionate tone that is both perfectly delightful and boldly antiromantic. I do not sense that any lines in this poem or in any of the other poems to Stella allow the conclusion that a marriage took place.

Poems for Fun

We are on safer ground when we look at another type of poetry. Swift very often versified for fun; and, since this aspect of his work deserves illustration, I have from a large store selected and will present without comment, four samples. Swift called them "family trifles."[21]

As Thomas was cudgelld one day by his Wife,
He took to the Street, and fled for his Life,
Tom's three dearest Friends came by in the
    Squabble
And sav'd him at once from the Shrew and the
    Rabble;
Then ventur'd to give him some sober Advice,
But Tom is a Person of Honor so nice,
Too wise to take Council, too proud to take
    Warning,
That he sent to all three a Challenge next
    morning.
Three Duels he fought, thrice ventu'd his Life
Went home, and was cudgell'd again by his Wife.
              (no title; 1723?)

    The Servant's Maxim
    Eat like a Turk
       Sleep like a Dormouse;
    Be last at Work,
       At Victuals foremost.
       (1725)

Written by the Reverend Dr. Swift On His own Deafness
Deaf, giddy, helpless, left alone,
To all my Friends a Burthen grown,
No more I hear my Church's Bell,
Than if it rang out for my Knell:
At Thunder now no more I start,
Than at the Rumbling of a Cart:
Nay, what's incredible, alack!
I hardly hear a Woman's Clack.
              (1734)

    From *Apollo's Edict*
    No Simile shall be begun,
    With *rising* or with *setting* Sun . . .
    No Son of mine shall dare to say,
    Aurora usher'd in the Day.
        (ll. 12–13, 20–21;
    understandably attributed to Swift.
    Undated. First printed, 1728)

"Never any one liveing thought like you": "Cadenus and Vanessa"

"Cadenus and Vanessa," "regarded by some as the finest of Swift's metrical pieces,"[22] is too long to quote here in full. The poem gives a sort of immortality to Esther Vanhomrigh, the young London lady who had fallen in love with Swift. Written for her in 1713, and probably revised later, the poem was not published until 1726, three years after her death. When he wrote the poem, Swift (Cadenus) was in his middle forties, and Esther (Vanessa) in her early twenties (she was born in 1687 or 1688). The relationship between them became very complicated and even dangerous for Swift when Vanessa indicated that her happiness required the then newly appointed dean of St. Patrick's Cathedral in Dublin to change his role from mentor and family friend—and at least *that* we were sure he was—to lover. Swift was "at an age," wrote Samuel Johnson, "when vanity is strongly excited by the amorous attention of a young woman."[23] This may be so; it often is. In any event, he appears to have been neither skillful nor kind in the way he handled the lovelorn lady.

"Cadenus and Vanessa" begins like a true pastoral:

> The Shepherds and the Nymphs were seen
> Pleading before the Cyprian Queen.
> The Council for the Fair began,
> Accusing that False Creature, Man.
>
> (ll. 1–4)

But the real intention of this pastoral soon becomes clear. As Professor Quintana says, the purpose is to smooth over an awkward situation by resolving "all difficulties into high comedy."[24] Swift (Cadenus = *Decanus* [Latin for *dean*]) speaks in his own person:

> Vanessa, not in Years a Score,
> Dreams of a Gown of forty-four;
> Imaginary Charms can find,
> In Eyes with Reading almost blind;
> Cadenus now no more appears
> Declin'd in Health, advanc'd in Years.
> She fancies Musick in his Tongue
> Nor further looks, but thinks him young.
> What Mariner is not afraid,

> To venture in a Ship decay'd?
> What Planter will attempt to yoke
> A Sapling with a falling Oak?
>
> (ll. 524–35)

The questions asked are sensible, but the tone that Swift gives the lines vitiates their clearheadedness. Where the situation probably called for a certain amount of unflappable ruthlessness on Swift's part, it received only the arch raillery of "high comedy."

Another coyly suggestive stanza refers to Vanessa's pursuit of her dean:

> But what Success Vanessa met,
> Is to the World a Secret yet:
> Whether the Nymph, to please her Swain,
> Talks in a high Romantick Strain:
> Or whether he at last descends
> To like with less Seraphick Ends;
> Or, to compound the Business, whether
> They temper Love and Books together;
> Must never to Mankind be told,
> Nor shall the conscious Muse unfold.
>
> (ll. 818–27)

The Queen of Love finally adjudicates this ambiguous and perplexing case: she "Decreed the Cause against the Men" (l. 851). It is not clear exactly what her decree amounted to; perhaps she should have been more specific and decreed against "the Man" named Swift. Samuel Johnson's censure seems to be in this instance not unfair: "[R]ecourse must be had to that extenuation which [Swift] so much despised, 'men are but men'. . . . [N]o other honest plea can be found, that he delayed a disagreeable discovery from time to time, dreading the immediate bursts of distress, and watching for a favorable moment."[25] Apparently the "favorable moment" was never found, for the persistent Vanessa followed her dean to Ireland; there she lingered and languished, "baffled and embittered,"[26] until her death in 1723. Even before her death, however, the relationship between them for some reason had ended.

The rupture occurred in the summer of 1722,[27] but the reason for the break must be added to the list of mysteries surrounding Swift's life. Sometimes of the mystery and much of the bitterness and baffle-

ment of this tragic story is dramatically illustrated by one of Vanessa's
letters to Swift, written about two years before her death:

How many letters must I send you before I shall receive an answer [?] can you
deny me in my misery the only comfort which I can expect at present [?] oh
that I could hope to see you here . . . I was born with violent passions which
terminate all in one that unexpressible passion I have for you consider the
killing emotions which I feel from your neglect of me and shew some tenderness for me or I shall lose my senses . . . I firmly believe could I know your
thoughts (which no humane creature is capable of gueussing at because never
any one liveing thought like you) I should find you have often in a rage wished
me religious hopeing then I should have paid my devotions to heaven but that
would not spair you for was I an Enthusiast still you'd be the Deity I should
worship. . . .[28]

Two years after this letter was written Vanessa was dead. Though a
woman of some wealth, in her will she left nothing to Swift. His name
was not even mentioned.

That manuscript copies of Swift's poem to Vanessa were in circula-
tion for years before the poem was published is indicated by Swift's
letter to Knightley Chetwode (19 April 1726) in which he said, "I am
very indifferent what is done with ["Cadenus and Vanessa"], for printing cannot make it more common than it is."[29] Nothing can tell us
whether the "indifference" was real, easily assumed, or painfully forced.
We must conclude, therefore, that "Cadenus and Vanessa" remains a
tantalizing and ambiguous human document, whatever a reader thinks
of it as poetry. I like Joseph Horrell's comment: the poem is "an elegant
piece of persiflage."[30] And David Downie has recently cautioned us,
stringently but I think fairly, that since this very personal poem was
originally intended for Vanessa's eyes only, it "must not be overbur-
dened with the weight of serious statements it was not designed to
carry, less it sink without a trace."[31]

The pastoral cast of "Cadenus and Vanessa" seems to me significant:
there is a strong likelihood that Swift was hiding behind it. The
unhappy drama that the poem depicts might not have ended tragically
if he had dealt as openly and as realistically with the real-life "swain"
(himself) and the living "nymph" (Vanessa) as he dealt with Dermot
and Sheelah in another of his poems, the "Pastoral Dialogue" of 1729.
In this lively spoofing of the pastoral tradition, an older—and finally in
this instance wiser—Swift begins, tongue in cheek: "Sing heavenly
Muse in sweetly flowing Strain, / The soft Endearments of the Nymph

and Swain." As the two lovers peel potatoes together, Dermot is moved
to express himself as follows:

> When you saw Tady at Long-bullets play,
> You sat and lows'd him all the Sun-shine Day.
> How could you, Sheelah, listen to his Tales,
> Or crack such Lice as his betwixt your Nails?
>
> (ll. 33–36)

Sheelah replies:

> When you with Oonah stood behind a Ditch,
> I peept, and saw you kiss the dirty Bitch.
> Dermot, how could you touch those nasty Sluts!
> I almost wisht this Spud were in your Guts.
>
> (ll. 37–40)

Dermot extricates himself: "If I ever touch [Oonah's] Lips again, / May
I be doom'd for Life to weed in Rain." And all ends happily with
Dermot's passionate declaration: "O, could I earn for thee, my lovely
lass, / A pair of Brogues to bear thee dry to Mass!" Altogether, the
conversation bespeaks an attachment which, though stormy, was yet
honest. What needed to be said was said; thus the relationship was less
calculated to produce the inevitable heartache than the real-life counter-
part so elegantly obfuscated in "Cadenus and Vanessa."

Lampoons

In 1816 in the *Edinburgh Review* the Scottish critic Francis Jeffrey
said of Swift: "He was, without exception, the greatest and most effi-
cient libeller that ever exercised the trade; and possessed, in an eminent
degree, all the qualifications which it requires:—a clear head—a cold
heart—a vindictive temper— . . . and a complete familiarity with
every thing that is low, homely, and familiar in language."[32] Jeffrey
was a trifle severe, but it is true that Swift was a truly great hater and
that he wrote a number of outspoken and sometimes quite cruel verse
lampoons. Targets might be Queen Anne's favorite, the red-haired
duchess of Somerset (see "The Windsor Prophecy"); or King George II;
or Prime Minister Sir Robert Walpole; or John Sharp, the archbishop of
York; they might be a great English general, or merely some Irish
Yahoo-types (see "The Legion Club") who were not behaving them-

selves, politically. The range is wide. How vicious Swift could be when he felt himself strongly in the right is well illustrated by his "Satirical Elegy on the Death of a Late Famous General." This poem is Swift's biting requiescat in pace to the great Whig general, the duke of Marlborough. He was no doubt a hero to many people even while Swift was attacking him. After all, he had brought brilliant military victories and glory to his country. This being so, why did "some folks think, / He left behind *so great a s{tin}k*"? (ll. 15–16). He "stank," the poem reminds us, because, while bringing titles and a fortune to himself, he brought misery and death to uncounted numbers of his countrymen. He therefore deserved the final reward that Swift accorded him: a return to the "dirt" which was his origin.

> His Grace! impossible! What dead!
> Of old age too, and in his bed
> And could that Mighty Warrior fall?
> And so inglorious, after all!
>
> . . . .
>
> And could he be indeed so old
> As by the news-papers we're told?
> Threescore, I think, is pretty high?
> 'Twas time in conscience he should die.
> This world he cumber'd long enough;
> He burnt his candle to the snuff;
> And that's the reason, some folks think,
> He left behind *so great a s——k.*
>
> . . . .
>
> Let pride be taught by this rebuke
> How very mean a thing's a Duke;
> From all his ill-got honours flung,
> Turn'd to that dirt from whence he sprung.
>   (ll. 1–4; 9–16; 29–32) (1722)

Because Swift was himself so much in his writings—in contrast to the aesthetic distance maintained by Pope—his critics often confine their comments exclusively to him and say nothing about the poem or prose passage in question. We may recall, as illustration, Thackeray's notorious lines: "Would you have liked to be a friend of the great Dean? . . . If you had been his inferior in parts . . . , he would have bullied, scorned, and insulted you; if, undeterred by his great reputation, you had met him like a man, he would have quailed before you, . . . and years after written a foul epigram about you—watched for you in a sewer, and come out to assail you with a coward's blow and a dirty bludgeon. . . ."[33] Jeffry's and Thackery's criticisms are typical of those that attacked Swift as a man. I take them really as a kind of commentary on the power of what Swift wrote. It must be admitted that the "Satirical Elegy" on Marlborough is, as Harold Williams says, an "ungenerous attack."[34] But the comment is relevant as criticism in that it reflects a measure of the tremendous impression left by the poem. I suspect that what Harold Williams felt was the same sort of impact that most readers must feel: from the first to the last line, with the terrible word *dirt,* this poem is a statement that, for concentrated venom and pure vindictiveness, is as lethal as anything in our language. Though we need not cherish it for this reason, I believe we should respect it. It brilliantly achieves what its author intended it to achieve.

"The Day of Judgement"

The date of composition of this poem is not known, though Williams puts it, tentatively, at 1731.[35] This date seems reasonable enough, especially if we can agree that a person's writing may be presumed to be affected by the times he lives in and his sense of well-being—or lack thereof—in his own life at the time of composition. In his thirties, Swift was frustrated and had reason to be disappointed and bitter: the *Tale* volume reflects this fact. In his middle fifties Swift had established himself as a powerful dean and an Irish hero: as a consequence *Gulliver's Travels,* however corrosive its satire, has seemed to be not as despairing as is the earlier *Tale* volume. In the early 1730s, however, when Swift was in his sixties, the oscillation across the spectrum of bitterness and despair swerved hard again toward an extreme. As Landa tells us, "from 1730, Swift's tone grew sharper, his hopelessness more apparent."[36] The reason for this shift may have been his growing conviction that all his hopes for preserving his church and his Ireland were doomed to failure. He wrote to Pope at this time, "[Without] a miracle we are at our last gasp. . . ." And earlier in this same letter, its author had dourly observed that "The common saying of life being a Farce is true in every sense but the most important one, for it is a ridiculous tragedy. . . ."[37] The loss of Stella (d. 1728) and of his great clerical supporter, Archbishop King (d. 1729), no doubt were contributing factors to Swift's lowness of spirits. "The Day of Judgement" may thus be read as, at least to some extent, a reflection of this extreme lowness of spirits.

"The Day of Judgement" is a short account of a dream. In it, the narrator sees and hears Jove (supreme among the Gods) thunder his condemnation of us all:

> "Offending Race of Human Kind,
> "By Nature, Reason Learning, blind;
> (ll. 11–12).

Jove concludes:

> "The World's mad Business Now is o'er
> "And I resent [your] Pranks no more
> "I to such Blockheads set my Wit!
> "I damn such Fools! Go, go, you're bit"
> (ll. 19–22).

This is our dreamer's "horrid vision" (1.3) of what happens when humankind stands, "amazed, confus'd" (l. 7), before Jove's throne and awaits the supreme god's judgment. The judgment is that man is a fool; man is damned; Jove has "had it" with him.

Like all Swift's most memorable works, this one is "Free from all tricks and peculiarities[;] it holds to its purpose with absolute directness and lucidity."[38] The words are those of Sir Henry Craik and are surely applicable to this stern and forbidding proclamation.

The "Unprintable" Poems

During the early 1730s Swift wrote a number of so-called unprintable poems. The best-known of these are "The Lady's Dressing Room" (1730), "Strephon and Chloe" (1731), "A Beautiful Young Nymph Going to Bed" (1731), and "Cassinus and Peter" (1731). In the first of these the lovely Celia "sh–ts"; in the second one Chloe, in her wedding bed, has to reach for the chamber pot in order to "p––s"; in the last one "Celia, Celia[,] Celia sh–––." The language is not new to Swift's writings at this time. But these poems do indicate a heightened and intensified concern with such matters. Why the seemingly increased concern? Conventional biographers might see some explanation in some of the facts I have mentioned above: Swift was coming into his mid-sixties; Vanessa was long dead (1723); Stella had died in 1728; and when Archbishop King, "The Ancient hero," died in 1729 Swift lost his strongest support in his efforts to help Ireland. All the causes he had worked for seemed to be moving in the wrong direction. His letter to Pope, cited above, reveals his despair. In a letter to Lady Suffolk he wrote again about Ireland as he saw it at this time: it was a hopeless situation. "I would not," he said, "prescribe a dose for the dead."[39]

Do these biographical facts explain the 1730 to 1733 series of scatological poems? I would hesitate to make a judgment. David Nokes is no doubt right, however, when he asserts that they "have done more to blacken [Swift's] reputation with later generations than anything else he wrote."[40] Our psychoanalytical critics, and those sympathetic with their positions, remind us about what, as Norman Brown tells us, "Any reader of Jonathan Swift knows": "In his analysis of human nature there is an emphasis on, and attitude toward, the anal function that is unique in Western literature."[41] Dr. Brown singles out the poems I have named above as scandalous examples of this fact.

As we have seen, Swift's concern with filth, anal or otherwise, is not limited to the scatological poems but is seen off and on pretty much through all his writing career. According to a number of critics— Phyllis Greenacre, Norman Brown, Irvin Ehrenpreis, and David Nokes might be mentioned—this persistent concern, as well as many of Swift's other problems, can be explained by his loss of both parents in his infancy. Brown writes with great confidence: "Swift lost his father before he was born; was kidnapped from his mother only three years later, only to be abandoned by his mother one month after his return to her at the psychoanalytically crucial Oedipal period. By psychoanalytical standards such a succession of infantile traumata must establish more than a predisposition to life long neurosis."[42]

All the above information, biographical and psychoanalytical, forms part of a backdrop that may be valuable to some readers as we look carefully at one poem, representative of these "unprintables." Readers will get from this backdrop, according to their bent, varying degrees of help.

The particular poem I have in mind is "A Beautiful Young Nymph Going to Bed" (1731). It should no longer be shrugged off as merely "nasty, noxious, disgusting, and painful."[43] In matters of taste and criticism the winds blow freely these days and one valuable consequence of this freedom is that obscenity in a poem does not necessarily either qualify it for or disqualify it from serious critical attention.

In a "Beautiful Young Nymph" Swift adopted a device better known from its appearance in book 2 of *Gulliver's Travels:* in the boudoir of a female, or group of females, he set a loose-tongued narrator (like Gulliver among the Brobdingnagian ladies-in-waiting) who later told everybody everthing he saw. This "everything" could sometimes be quite offensive to the narrator's audience; an instance is recorded by Swift's friend, Mrs. Pilkington, who wrote that her old mother threw up her dinner when she heard "The Lady's Dressing Room."[44]

Swift's device was as monstrously unfair to women as it would have been to any person similarly depicted. But his point is clear enough: he simply did not believe in nymphs. Here as usual he seems to be asking for an honest description of what is seen. So, if we must describe women, describe them as they are. Thus in an earlier poem, "To Stella" (1720), he writes,

> Should a Porter make Enquiries
> For Chloe, Sylvia, Phillis, Iris;
> Be told the Lodging, Lane and Sign,
> The Bow'rs that hold those Nymphs divine;
> Fair Chloe would perhaps be found
> With Footmen tippling under Ground,
> The charming Silvia beating Flax,
> Her Shou_ders mark'd with bloody Tracks;
> Bright Phillis mending ragged Smocks,
> And radiant Iris in the Pox.

The intention to record reality aright is laudable, even if the insistence that usually ignored facts must be considered led paradoxically to a kind of unreality. When facts conventionally ignored make up *the* picture, instead of *part* of the picture, distortion becomes inevitable. Moreover, when the distortion is wildly exaggerated, the result is caricature, which can be funny. Swift's "Beautiful Young Nymph" is caricature, but, though there certainly are comic details in the poem, the overall impression is not funny. It is not funny mainly because Swift feels so strongly both that what he sees is the terribly real whole truth of this situation and that this whole truth is quite horrible to comtemplate. Had the "Beautiful Young Nymph" been read to Mrs.

Pilkington's mother, I have no doubt that she would have had to throw up again. Here is how the poem begins:

> Corinna, Pride of Drury-Lane,
> For whom no Shepherd sighs in vain;
> Never did Covent Garden boast
> So bright a batter'd, strolling Toast;
> No drunken Rake to pick her up,
> No Cellar where on Tick to sup;
> Returning at the Midnight Hour;
> Four Stories climbing to her Bow'r;
> Then, seated on a three-legged Chair,
> Takes off her artificial Hair:
> Now, Picking out a Crystal Eye,
> She wipes it clean, and lays it by.
> Her Eye-Brows from a Mouse's Hyde,
> Stuck on with Art on either Side,
> Pulls off with Care, and first display 'em.
> Then in a Play-Book, smoothly lays 'em.
> (ll. 1–16)

And so on. The poem is truly wonderful and entirely relentless, both as parody of the too familiar "poetic" depiction of a "nymph" and as a limning of a filthy female (with perhaps even the nasty implication that an honest observer would find all females equally filthy). The degree of distortion in this caricature is sharply illuminated if we recall John Donne's management of much the same situation in his "To His Mistress Going to Bed":

> Off with that girdle, like heavens Zone glistering,
> But a far fairer world incompassing.
> Unpin that spangled breastplace which you wear,
> That th'eyes of busie fooles may be stopt there.
> . . . .
> Full nakedness! all joyes are due to thee, . . .

Swift's Corinna has a different look about her. She "Pulls out the rags contriv'd to prop / Her flabby dugs, and down they drop" (ll. 21–22). Then

> Up goes her Hand, and off she slips
> The Bolsters, that supply her Hips.

With gentlest Touch, she next explores
Her Chancres, Issues, running Sores.
                              (ll. 27–30)

The poem ends with these lines: "The Nymph, though in this mangled
Plight, / Must ev'ry Morn her Limbs unite. / . . . Who sees will spew;
who smells, be poisoned" (ll. 65–66; 74). If the last line had read,
"Who sees *should* spew," then the depiction of this poor prostitute
would have led us finally to, and in fact invited, moral censure. It
might even have allowed some pity. It does neither.

The poem contrasts instructively not only with Donne's "To His
Mistress Going to Bed," but also with Pope's "The Rape of the Lock."
The Belinda of Pope's poem is of a higher social level, but morally she
is on a par with Swift's Corinna. The significant differences, however,
are in the points of view and in the methods of the two poets. Pope is
far more the craftsman and far more the poet. His Belinda, getting
ready for the day, "Repairs her smiles," "awakens every grace," and—as
she continues with her cosmetics—"Sees by degrees a purer blush arise"
(the cheek with rouge on it is "purer" than the cheek with no makeup!). Working here for Pope is a brilliant and a believable metaphor:
like any fashionable belle, Belinda is restored to herself by what she
puts on. The metaphor shapes all the lovely innuendoes of this passage.
As an objective observer, Pope saw that what Belinda put on was by no
means, after all, quite so important as she thought it to be, if she ever
thought at all; but this he realized with a sardonic and even a kindly
tolerance.

Swift, on the other hand, was not an objective observer. In the
"Beautiful Young Nymph" he is not kind and he is not tolerant, and
because, to borrow two useful phrases from T. S. Eliot's *After Strange
Gods,* the "man who suffers" is rarely separate in this or in any of Swift's
poems from the "mind that creates," the result is that the man Swift is
always in his poems, caring very much that we understand what he sees
and thinks and hoping also very much that we understand what we
ought to see and think. Because he cared so much, he was compellingly
insistent that we wipe off Corinna's greasy façade and see her for the
dreadful bawd that she was. This concern was so urgent with him that
he could not be objective, he could not be kind, and he was even forced
into exaggeration. John Aden is almost exactly on the mark, I believe,
when he says that "Swift cannot alter the facts of Corinna's life; he can
only (at least he will only) show them and let them witness whatever

the pity of it is, the pity she's a whore."[45] I would have ended the sentence with "he can only (at least he will only) show them." I see no evidence of "pity."

Further, the figurative language of metaphor and symbol is used only in the most obvious sense in the "Beautiful Young Nymph," as in Swift's poems generally; and it is never used as a shaping principle for the whole (as Pope used it, with Belinda; or Swift himself, with the Lilliputians in *Gulliver's Travels*). As a consequence the "Beautiful Young Nymph" is typical of much of Swift's poetry in that it is more glaringly photographic than generative. This poem is, therefore, memorable mostly as a depiction of a squalid and dirty whore. The photographer is pleading merely that we look: *please look; only look. See this as it is.* "Who sees will spew."

Poetry as Talk

One final aspect of Swift's poetry deserves more explicit comment. Again like Pope, Swift had that great talent, often referred to, for re-creating dialogue. Maurice Johnson aptly points up this fact: "What there is to grin at in Swift's poetry often arises from characterization through monologue and dialogue ingeniously adapted to rhyme. His cookmaids, noblemen, idle wives, clergymen, bookdealers, and politicians speak unmistakably in voices of their own. They ramble or superciliously condescend, gabble, or protest in turn."[46]

What Williams calls the "everyday friendliness" of much of these familiar verses[47] is extremely attractive. Some of the verses, like the poems to Stella and the "Verses on the Death of Dr. Swift" attain poetic distinction, while other incidental pieces of various lengths addressed to Irish friends like the Rochforts or the Achesons, Sheridan or Delaney, reach no great heights as literature but are often entertaining and valuable source of information. For example, "Lady A-S-N" [Acheson], Weary of the Dean" (1728?) is not only a charming little poem, but also one of the few contemporary sources that tell us what Swift looked like. (Swift's puns in pig Latin, his epigrams, and the many little private jokes—all of which fit into this same category of familiar verse—need no critical comment.)

Probably Swift's best-known poem belongs in this category of familiar verse. The poem is entitled "Verses on the Death of Dr. Swift" and was "occasioned," said its author, "By reading a Maxim in Rochefoulcault": "In the Adversity of our best Friends, we find something that doth not displease us."

Early printings of this poem suffered excisions by other hands because some passages "might excite an accusation of vanity against the author, [and] . . . [other passages] are not accurate statements of fact."[48] Swift resented these changes in his text, as might be expected. Fortunately, a full and accurate text with Swift's own notes was finally published by Sir Harold Williams in his indispensable *The Poems of Jonathan Swift* (1937). The full version is almost five hundred lines long and quite consistently demonstrates Swift's happy talent of putting good talk into good verse. As Samuel Johnson remarked of Shakespeare in his *Preface to Shakespeare* (1765), "the dialogue is on a level with life." The conversational lilt and the easy and seemingly effortless control of rhythm and rhyme show Swift, the poet, in one of his more expert and certainly most appealing roles. As witty talk, the poem is unsurpassed in the canon of his verse.

The tone and character of this poem can be suggested by this excerpt:

> My female Friends, whose tender Hearts
> Have better learn'd to act their Parts,
> Receive the News in doleful Dumps,
> "The Dean is dead, (and what is Trumps?)
> "Then Lord have Mercy on his Soul.
> "(Ladies I'll venture for the Vole.)
> "Six Deans they say must bear the Pall.
> "(I wish I knew what King to call.)
> "Madam, your Husband will attend
> "The Funeral of so good a Friend.
> "No Madam, 'tis a shocking Sight,
> "And he's engag'd Tomorrow Night!
> "My Lady Club wou'd take it ill,
> "If he shou'd fail her at Quadrill.
> "He lov'd the Dean. (I lead a Heart.)
> "But dearest Friends, they say, must part.
> "His Time was come, he ran his Race;
> "We hope he's in a better Place.
>   (ll. 225–242)

In its themes and in its tone, "Verses on the Death of Dr. Swift" are consistent with opening comments by and about Rochfoucault: "In the Adversity of our best Friends, we find something that doth not displease us" and "As Rochefoucault his Maxims drew / From Nature, I believe 'em true" (ll. 1–2).

Early on in this poem the writer depicts himself as not unlike his friends. "I have no Title to aspire," he says, "Yet when you sink, I seem the higher" (ll. 45–46). Thus he too, jealous of a friend's rise, is not unhappy to learn of his fall. It is self-interest that motivates him and everybody else, as instance after instance in this poem demonstrates. The self-interest is reflected in the callous behavior of the card-playing friends with "tender hearts" who casually dismiss him: "The Dean is dead, (and what is Trumps?)"; and it has even contaminated the "Gracious, Mild and Good" Queen who, hearing of the Dean's demise, says, "He's dead you say; why let him rot" (l. 183).

No great problems of interpretation are posed as the poem progresses ironically, though by no means bitterly, through the first three hundred or so lines. For the modern reader, however, the final lines (ll. 307–484) have presented something of a puzzle. They also puzzled, or at least bothered, those early and unauthorized editors who excised the many lines (usually about a third of the poem) that might otherwise have "[excited] an accusation of vanity against the author." Here are some lines which do still—though I think wrongly—excite readers to accusations of vanity and inaccuracy:

"To steal a Hint was never known,
"But what he writ was all his own."

(ll. 317–18)

"He never courted Men in Station,

. . . .

"Because he sought for no Man's Aid."

(ll. 305, 328)

"Fair LIBERTY was all his Cry;
"For her he stood prepar'd to die."

(ll. 347–48)

". . . Power was never in his Thought;
"And, Wealth he valued not a Grout."

(ll. 355–56)

"Perhaps I may allow, the Dean
"Had too much Satyr in his Vein;"

. . . .
"Yet, Malice never was his Aim;
"He lash'd the Vice but spar'd the Name."
                              (ll. 455–56; 459–60)

"[He] was chearful to his dying Day."
                              (l. 477)

All of the above quotations are distortions, if not downright falsifications, of the facts. David Nokes's response is typical of what some
biographers say: "Much of what Swift claims for himself [in "Verses on
the Death of Dr. Swift"] is both vain and false."[49] The reaction by
Nokes is understandable enough, if it is assumed that Swift is himself
the speaker in these quotations.

Given the introduction by Rochefoucault and given Swift's own
remarks about him, we look for and get page after page of wry, sardonic, witty descriptions and commentary. We also get, toward the
end of the poem, a number of observations (like those cited above) that
seem to show a self-interested Swift in a series of outrageous posturings
and guilty of misstating facts. The important point to remember here,
however, is that Swift was not the "speaker" in these quotations. He
was clever enough to cause all of them to be spoken by an objective
observer. "Suppose me dead," Swift had written, "and then suppose / A
Club assembled at the *Rose;* / Where from Discourse of this and that, / I
grow the subject of their Chat. . . ." Then "One quite indiff'rent in
the Cause, / My Character impartial draws" (ll. 299–302; 305–6). The
voice in the entire remainder of the poem is this objective persona. All
the distortions, exaggerations, and falsifications are the observations of
this so-called impartial observer at the "Club" meeting in "the Rose."
All the distortions and false statements are thus not Swift's but those of
his friend at the club.

Richard Rodino suggests that "The exaggerated encomium in the
second half of the poem is meant to evoke, and thereby 'prove,' the
universal jealousy and self-interest predicted in the first half of the
poem."[50] This is very good. The comment reinforces our sense of the
structural and thematic unity of the poem. On reflection, however,
perhaps we can say that the "vain and false" remarks do more than just
"prove" the thesis Swift asserted in the first part of the poem. Even in
these distortions Swift put in the mouth of his friend at the club, we
must note some truths. For example he was in fact true to his (limited)

idea of "fair LIBERTY"; he did hate to court "men in station" (though he often enough did so); and I am convinced that the actions he lashed were generally his primary concern, not the agents of those actions. In short, I believe that one of the final ironies of this delightful poem is that, in the last and sometimes maligned third of the poem, a depiction of Swift as hero emerges and that our author slyly enjoyed watching that picture take form. David Vieth is exactly on the right track, therefore, when he says that what seems to be Swift's self-praise "gains our assent so far as it fits our preconceived notions of Swift's identity. Above all, this is Swift the national hero, the 'Swift' of Yeats, Joyce, and Beckett."[51] The depiction may not—in fact, does not—bespeak the literal truth. It is what Richard Feingold calls "a composition of plainly sign-posted distortions and exaggerations . . . [attributed] to a figure [that Swift] describes as impartial and reliable!" but the figure shaped by these distortions turns out to be a "triumphantly declarative self-portrait" of Swift himself.[52]

"Verses on the Death of Dr. Swift" is a great pleasure to come upon. I enjoy the many ironies. I like the famous "satiric touch" at the end.

> "He [Swift] gave the little Wealth he had,
> "To build a House for Fools and Mad:
> "And shew'd by one satyric Touch,
> "No Nation Wanted it so much:
> "That Kingdom he hath left his Debtor,
> "I wish it soon may have a Better.

The poem is an entertaining and masterly example of the "everyday friendliness" of Swift's familiar verse.

Conclusion

Like John Greenleaf Whittier, Swift in his maturity had no illusions about his poetry. Whittier's conclusion was that "I should not dare to warrant any of my work for a long drive," and "I am not one of the master singers and don't pose as one."[53] Swift's self-judgment was, "I have been only a Man of Rhymes, and that upon Trifles. . . ."[54] And at the end of his poem called a "Left-handed Letter to Dr. Sheridan" (1718), he added, "I beg your Pardon for using my left Hand, but I was in great Haste, and the other Hand was employed at the same Time in writing some Letters of Business."[55] However much else is involved, the artist who takes himself too seriously or who uses his talents wrongly—as Swift did in his odes written during the Moor Park years—or who fails to take his work seriously enough does not usually attain first ranking. Swift is not one of our greatest poets. But he was a true poet. We should not forget that, besides numerous versified riddles and epigrams, he wrote more than two hundred and fifty poems. Many of them were to be sure merely casual and spontaneous productions but a very fair share were studied productions, like "Verses on the Death of Dr. Swift," which repay our reading. I certainly cannot join Samuel Johnson in such a near dismissal of his poetry as this: "In the Poetical Works of Dr. Swift there is not much upon which the critick can excercise his powers."[56]

To answer the question, "What is poetry?" in terms that will include Swift is not my intention here. For the modern reader the major problem with Swift's poetry is obvious enough, however: he must accommodate himself to the truth that some very endearing poetic traditions find absolutely no expression in Swift's poetry. The sort of exultation that Bach or Mozart put into music, or that Keats put into verse, would, I suspect, have merely embarrassed Swift, even if his experience of and in the world had given him anything much to exult about. It had not. Furthermore, if we believe the doctrine current in some circles today, that what is stated is not literature and what is not stated is truth, then Swift is not, in his poetry, a literary figure at all. He stated. Or if we agree with T. S. Eliot that "the more perfect the artist, the more completely separate in him will be the man who suffers and the mind which creates,"[57] we will have to agree that Swift comes very far from perfection. In his poetry there is no such separation. His poems are enormously, and for the most part immediately, revealing statements of what was in his heart and on his mind.

Swift's poems are, at their best, like the man himself: bright and clever; strong; sometimes very wise; and often very disturbing. They do occasionally distort reality in its difficult passage into words, but the distortion is generally in a healthy direction. That their author also had, and demonstrated, the "Kind of Knack at Rhyme" that elevated itself into some memorable poetry is merely the happiest kind of bonus.

Chapter Five
Cathedral Dean and Patriot

About midway through his long exile from England, Swift told Bolingbroke that, unless he left Ireland, he would die there "like a poisoned rat in a hole."[1] He never received the English appointment that would have led him to leave Ireland permanently, and he did die in Ireland—but more a national hero than "a poisoned rat." Nonetheless, the cheerful and confident note that in earlier years marked much of *The Journal to Stella* became increasingly less often heard as the years had passed. Because his love of fun rarely deserted him for long, he was able to report in a letter to John Gay and the duchess of Queensbury (10 July 1732) that his "rule" of life was "*Vive la bagatelle!*"[2] But probably more characteristic of these later years was the remark he made in a letter of 1729: "I never wake without finding life a more insignificant thing than it was the day before."[3] Much of the later prose (though happily not all) is somber in mood.

In a revealing comment to Pope (10 January 1721) Swift said: "In a few weeks after the loss of that excellent Princess [Queen Anne], I came to my station here; where I have continued ever since in the greatest privacy, and utter ignorance of those events which are commonly talked of in the world. . . . I had indeed written some Memorials of the four last years of the Queen's reign. . . . [Also] I have written in this kingdom, a discourse to persuade the wretched people to wear their own Manufactures instead of those from England: This Treatise soon spread very fast, being agreeable to the sentiments of the whole nation. . . ."[4]

In this significant letter Swift not only described his drab years following the death of Queen Anne in 1714, the fall of the Tory party soon afterwards, and his return to Dublin; he also signaled the beginning of an astounding time of creativity. Despite claims about his "privacy" and his "utter ignorance . . . of events . . . commonly talked of," the period in fact found him active and productive in his world. The 1720s began with *The Letter To a Young Gentleman Lately Entered into Holy Orders* and *A Proposal for the Universal Use of Irish Manufacture;* it continued with *A Letter to a Young Lady* (1723), *The*

Drapier Letters (1724–25), *Gulliver's Travels* (1726), and *A Modest Proposal* (1729)—to mention only the most outstanding prose works, and to say nothing whatsoever about the many good poems.

The Letter to a Young Gentleman Lately Entered into Holy Orders

The Letter to a Young Gentleman was dated 9 January 1720, and was purportedly written "By a Person of Quality." Apparently not directed to any specific person,[5] it is actually a sort of vest-pocket handbook for all preachers, especially young ones. In addition, and incidentally, it is useful as an introduction to Jonathan Swift, D.D., Dean of St. Patrick's Cathedral. In the *Letter* it is as usual important to be alert, however, to distinctions between Swift and the character he creates to do the narrating for him. Furthermore, if the narrator (a persona) is used, then it is important to establish Swift's attitude toward him. These two responsibilities are easily discharged by a reader of this *Letter*.

Swift depicts his writer as a knowledgeable, very sober lay person, fairly well along in life, with many clerical friends; also this poor fellow apparently has total recall of all the bad sermons he has ever heard. He is direct and clear in what he wants to say: "My Design in this Paper was not so much to instruct you in your business, either as a Clergyman, or a Preacher, as to warn you against some Mistakes. . . ." So dignified, sensible, and forthright a character Swift must have approved of and wanted us to listen to with respect.

His intention stated, our narrator begins immediately to make specific recommendations. He advises the young preacher to heed his style (style is defined as "Proper Words in proper Places"); to avoid "hard Words" (some of them, like *Attribute* and *Excentrick,* have long since passed into common use, though perhaps with different spellings); to refrain from *reading* [Swift's emphasis] his sermons to the congregation; to reject the temptation to be a wit ("it is very near a Million to One, that you have none"); to check any impulse to explain, and so eliminate, the mysteries of the Christian religion ("Providence intended there should be mysteries"); and, most of all, to appeal not to the passions of his people but to their understanding and reason ("I do not see how this Talent of moving the Passions, can be of any great Use towards directing Christian men in the Conduct of their Lives").

Our lay patron, as the narrator is termed on the title page of the

1720 Dublin edition, recounts an anecdote to enforce his last directive: "A Lady asked him, coming out of Church, whether it were not a very moving Discourse? Yes, said he, I was extremely sorry, for the Man is my Friend." Behind the narrator, Swift's sardonic voice is crystal clear. This same voice unremittingly for a lifetime derided and despised the "moving discourse" of fanatics, like Jack in *A Tale of a Tub,* wherever their characteristically undisciplined voices were heard.

The concluding section of this letter deals with "the frequent Custom of preaching against Atheism, Deism, [and] Free Thinking. . . ." The letter writer disapproves of such preaching. His premises accepted, his protests are as powerful now as they were then. He insists that "Reasoning will never make a Man correct an ill Opinion, which by Reasoning he never acquired." He protests that atheistical writings are a symptom of corruption in the nation, not a cause of it. He observes that a civilized state is one that includes learning and religion. The "Young Gentleman Lately Entered into Holy Orders" is given, finally, this cryptic no-nonsense decree: "the two principal Branches of Preaching, are first to tell the People what is their Duty; and then to convince them that it is so." This is sage counsel for a young preacher then or a young preacher now.

In a pessimistic mood, Swift was capable of giving quite different counsel. His "Advice to a Parson. An Epigram" (1723) cynically answers a question:

> Wou'd you rise in the Church, be Stupid and Dull,
> Be empty of Learning, of Insolence full[?]
> Tho' Lewd and Immoral, be Formal and Grave,
> In Flatt'ry an Artist, in Fawning a Slave,
> No Merit, no Science, no Virtue is wanting
> In him, that's accomplish'd in Cringing and Canting. . . .

The Sermons

Fortunately, Swift did not himself follow his "Advice to a Parson." It is a great deal more likely that he tried to heed his own lay patron's counsel in *The Letter to a Young Gentleman Lately Entered into Holy Orders.* For Swift, ordained priest in 1695, thereafter gave nearly half a century of active service to his church; and all the evidence says that he took his work as a dean and as a preacher very seriously. Hawkesworth repeats the somewhat mawkish tale purportedly derived from Swift very early in his clerical career: "He hoped that by diligent and constant application he should so far excel that the sexton might sometimes be asked on a Sunday morning, 'Pray does the doctor preach today?' "[6] The story, if true, is not inconsistent with the fact that Swift's deepest interest in the church was more temporal than spiritual, or even doctrinal.[7] Abundant evidence also demonstrates that, though Swift often scorned those who were concerned only with professional advancement and would go to any length to obtain it, sore annoyed was *he* without it.[8] Nonetheless, despite personal frustration and at last the disillusionment expressed in his letter in 1736 to Charles Ford ("I have long given up all hopes of Church or Christianity"[9]), he took very seriously his responsibilities as the dean, or chief administrative officer, of his cathedral and was regarded as effective in discharging those responsibilities. He had a full share—and perhaps more than his full share—of problems, conflicts, and enemies, probably because he was so conscientious; and also because, as John Lyon, a prebendary at St. Patrick's Cathedral and manager of Swift's affairs in his last years, said, "Dr. Swift knew the rights and jurisdiction of his place very well . . . and would not suffer any encroachments thereupon by any person whatsoever."[10]

A valuable source of information about Swift as dean is Louis Landa's *Swift and the Church of Ireland.* One of Landa's concluding observations about Swift as a dean is this: "Week after week he presided over chapter meetings in which the detailed business of the cathedral received attention—the approval of a lease, a decision to repair the fabric, the purchase of new prayer books, the replacement of a verger. Not even Swift's enemies accused him of neglecting his stewardship of St. Patrick's; and all of the early biographers testify to his scrupulous and pious management."[11]

As dean, Swift was expected to do his share of preaching, and he did so. Judging from his extant sermons I cannot say he was by our terms an exemplary spiritual leader, since he showed little interest in spiritual matters. There seems to be no doubt, however, that in his preaching he was dutiful and sincere in the always demanding performance of this aspect of his position and that in fact his listeners were pleased with him.

Unfortunately, most of his few extant sermons (there are only eleven we can be sure of) read like "pamphlets"—an epithet which Mrs. Pilkington and Dr. Delaney record that Swift himself applied to them.[12] Inclined to belittle these productions, he once wrote to his old friend from Kilroot, the Reverend John Winder: "Those sermons [written by Swift] You have thought fitt to transcribe will utterly disgrace You. . . . They were what I was firmly resolved to burn and especially some of them the idlest trifling stuff that ever was written, calculated for a Church without a company or a roof. . . ."[13] This degree of self-deprecation is not justified, for the sermons, if not great literature, are surely not mere "trifling stuff."

But though better written than his early odes, the sermons are today probably just about as rarely read. Like the odes, however, they reveal some of Swift's characteristic convictions. As an Anglican priest he could be expected to oppose doctrines and practices of the Roman Catholics, on the one side, and the Puritan dissenters, on the other. He would hold to the middle way—the *via media*—between these two extremes. His sermon "On the Trinity," "accords perfectly," Quintana tells us, "with rational faith as defined by those who preached the *via media.*"[14] He could be expected to attack dissenters ("Fanatics") with particular vigor: in "On Brotherly Love" he does so in a most "unbrotherly" and unloving way, even while in this same sermon holding to his middle way: "Let me earnestly exhort you to stand firm in your Religion, . . . without warping in the least, either to Popery on the one Side, or to Fanaticism on the other." He could be expected to reveal his distress about the Irish predicament: he does so in "Causes of the Wretched Condition of Ireland." He could be expected to allow into his sermons a share of his adamant opposition to the introduction into Ireland of Wood's halfpence. He does so with such strong statements as this: "When an open attempt is made, and far carried on, to make a great kingdom one large poor-house, . . . it is time for the pastor to cry out, that the wolf [Mr. Wood, that is] is getting into his flock, [and] to warn them to stand together . . . ("Doing Good"). Louis Landa writes, in sum, "[Swift's] views of charity, of foreign trade, of reason and the passions, of the Revolution of 1688, of England's treatment of Ireland—these and many others found their way into the sermons. . . . It may be said the sermons represent fairly adequately the range of his opinions."[15]

The early odes also refer to the evils that in the kingdom and in us lie (recall in the "Ode to Dr. William Sancroft" the comment that "Our British soil is over-rank, and breeds / Among the noblest flow'rs a thousand pois'nous weeds, / And ev'ry stinking weed . . . lofty grows" [ll. 101–3]; but the sermons identify these evils more specifically. In addition, for some people they might draw attention, these days, to a surprising and perhaps even disappointing aspect of Swift's thinking.

Specifically, some social critics of our times might be startled, and
perhaps even grieved, to discover among Swift's sermons such comments as those referred to in the quotations below. Here, for example,
is Swift's eighteenth-century version of that simplistic advice our twentieth century has seen on billboards: "Stop unemployment: Get a
Job!!": "Among the Number of those who beg in our Streets, or are
half-starved at Home, or languish in Prison for Debt, there is hardly
one in a hundred who doth not owe his Misfortune to his own Laziness
or drunkenness, or worse Vices. . . . Such Wretches . . . can only
blame themselves" ("On the Poor Man's Contentment" [undated]). The
same sermon presents one good reason why poor people should be
contented: "Their Rest is not disturbed by the Fear of Thieves and
Robbers." The following passage might serve as a paradigm for "blam-
ing the victim": "If we consider the many Misfortunes that befal private
Families, it will be found that Servants are the Causes and Instruments
of them all. Are our Goods embezzled, wasted, and destroyed? Is our
House burnt down to the Ground? It is by the Sloth, the Drunkenness
or the Villainy of Servants. Are we robbed and murdered in our beds? It
is by the Confederacy with our Servants" ("Causes of the Wretched
Condition of Ireland" [tentatively dated as sometime after 1720]).

Self-interest rules all. Rochefoucault had said so, and, in the sermon
cited immediately above, Swift agreed: "Human nature is so consti-
tuted, that we can never pursue any thing heartily but upon hopes of a
reward." In the following excerpt a Christian dean redefines the Parable
of the Good Samaritan: "If, by a small hurt and loss to myself, I can
procure a great good to my neighbour, in that case his interest is to be
preferred. For example, if I can be sure of saving his life, without great
danger to my own; if I can preserve him from being undone, without
ruining myself, . . . all this I am obliged to do . . ." ("Doing Good"
[1724]). Now hear an interesting footnote to the Golden Rule: "We
are, indeed, commanded to love our Neighbours as ourselves. . . . But
the copy doth not equal the original, so my neighbour cannot think it
hard, if I prefer myself, who am the original, before him, who is only
the copy" ("Doing Good" [1724]). This is the voice of our so often
ferocious genius whom we are used to seeing cut through to the heart of
things. Here, like the Babbitt of the Augustan Age, he is revealingly
and paradoxically telling us about his astonishing set of bourgeois
prejudices.

It is no news that Jonathan Swift was a conservative. In matters
theological and political, however, no body of his writing demonstrates

so fully and clearly as do the sermons the extent of his conservatism. In this respect they are valuable documents in the intellectual history of this great satirist.

It must be added, also, that contemporary evidence indicates that Swift was highly regarded as a preacher. He was the Anglican dean whom people loved as the Drapier; he was the Hibernian patriot on whose birthday they rang the church bells and built bonfires. John Lyon reminds us that when his friend preached, the cathedral was "well attended by a crowded audience."[16] Mrs. Pilkington, having attended a communion service at St. Patrick's, professed herself "charmed to see with what a becoming piety the dean performed that solemn service."[17] A little later (1755) Hawkesworth tells us that Swift was "a good priest. . . . He renewed the primitive practice of celebrating the holy communion every Sunday; and at this sacrament he was not only constantly present, but he consecrated and administered it with his own hands in a manner equally graceful and devout."[18]

Scholars and critics of our times are generally favorable in their comments. Ehrenpreis remarks that the sermons "that happen to be preserved are (nearly all of them) written with enough elegance and force to raise them above the work of all but the finest preachers of Swift's day."[19] Louis Landa would probably have joined Ehrenpreis in that assessment,[20] but Landa (like David Nokes, more recently) does express some reservations about Swift's sermons, especially about their lack of spiritual content.

Referring specifically to two sermons—"Upon the Excellence of Christianity" and "On the Testimony of Conscience"—Landa says, "Both are superficial." Commenting generally about the sermons, he concludes that they "are less profound and original than they are orthodox and conventional."[21] But after all, Swift's primary concern as dean was with the temporal affairs of his church, not with the spiritual.[22] David Nokes concludes with what he regards as the inescapable inference that "it was in his relationship with God that Swift felt most uneasy."[23] But Émile Pons, long before Nokes, had already said, "God is not One whose troublesome presence Swift had ever felt."[24]

To round out this discussion I will allude briefly to one sermon that exemplifies the various qualities I have noted about Swift the preacher. It is also the most lively of his sermons, and in fact it could as well be given as a lecture to a Rotary Club or any other organization that a speaker wants to entertain. The sermon begins with a cutting edge: "I have chosen these Words with Design, if possible, to disturb some Part in this Audience of half an Hour's Sleep, for the Convenience and Exercise whereof this Place, at this Season of the Day, is very much celebrated." Entitled "Upon Sleeping in Church" (undated), the sermon stands out not only as an able defense of the Cloth against unjust attack, but also as an effective indictment of behavior still existing in some churches. Swift concludes this memorable discourse with these words: "[Such] indecent Sloth is very much owing to that Luxury and Excess Men usually practice upon this Day, by which half the Service thereof is turned into Sin: Men dividing the Time between God and their Bellies, when after a gluttonous Meal, their Senses dozed and stupified, they retire to God's House to sleep out the Afternoon. Surely, Brethren, these Things ought not so to be."

Looking at the above sermon, I think we can fairly agree with Ehrenpreis's judgment that Swift was probably as good a preacher as most of those of his day. The sermons were well-organized and written by one of the best prose writers ever known. But though Swift must have preached hundreds of sermons, only twelve have ever been printed; and one of these twelve ("On the Difficulty of Knowing One's Self") may not be authentic. Happily there is no reason to think that the eleven remaining are not representative of all his sermons since they square so well with the ideas in the considerable body of his other works. Thus, though in fact there are some tantalizing gaps in our knowledge of the sermons, I see no reason to believe that their author ever strayed much from the advice he gave in *The Letter to a Young Gentleman Lately Entered into Holy Orders:* "Tell the People what is their duty; . . . convince them that it is so"; avoid "hard words"; put "proper words in proper places"; appeal not to the passions, but to reason. If the "reason" in Swift's sermons seems occasionally to be equated with bourgeois bias and Philistinism, and if never in his sermons is there "a hint of faith, or a whisper of a hope of salvation,"[25] we may be amazed—to paraphrase a famous passage in the "Digression on Madness"—to find these perhaps unsuspected faults under this one suit of clothes. But we need not despair, for—to continue with the paraphrase—as we proceed we shall not see the defects increase upon us either in number or in bulk. He remained a genius, whatever he wrote.

A Letter to a Young Lady on Her Marriage

The two most significant differences between *A Letter to a Young Lady* and the earlier *Letter to a Young Gentleman* are that Swift in *A Letter to a Young Lady* (written, 1723; first published, 1727) speaks in his own voice; and that he is known to have originally directed the letter quite specifically to one person in his cathedral city of Dublin: Deborah Staunton,[26] a young woman who had recently married a man "for some Years past my particular Favourite": John Rochfort.

The fifty-six-year-old dean attempts in this letter to advise a young woman who is just settling into marriage with the son of a family with which Swift had long been on friendly terms. At first glance, it might possibly seem that the new bride to whom the letter was sent must have had distinctly mixed emotions verging from gratitude to terror. The lady is told by the great dean to be modest in her deportment; to "abate a little of that violent Passion for fine Cloathes"; to be careful in matters of personal cleanliness ("For the satyrical part of mankind will needs believe, that it is not impossible to be very fine and very filthy"); to improve her mind by reading; to engage in intelligent conversation "in company with Men of learning" rather than to "consult with the Woman who sits next . . . about a new Cargo of Fans."

All this advice is the good, if run-of-the-mill, talk that a girl is always getting from her elders. We may assume that Deborah Staunton was polite enough to be grateful. But there are more surprising strokes. One is the wise suggestion about dress: let it be "one Degree lower than your Fortune can afford." Another is the insight, unusual coming from a man, that middle-aged women—visiting in the afternoon; playing cards at night—are usually regarded with a particularly harsh and virulent contempt by "the younger Part of their own Sex," (perhaps that is something he learned from Stella). Such counsel and such insights will no doubt cause a number of men to agree with Lord Orrery's remark: "This Letter ought to be read by all new married women, and will be read with pleasure and advantage by the most distinguished and accomplished ladies."[27]

Louis Landa has remarked that "[This] is a very charming letter welcoming to the Deanery circle a very young lady, whose parents and husband were alike Swift's particular friends."[28] To some readers, however, the letter has seemed to be a puzzling kind of "welcome" "to the Deanery circle" or to any circle at all. Does she need to be reminded to bathe regularly? Must she be informed so flatly, now, that a wise man "soon grows weary of acting the Lover"? Must she be warned "against the least Degree of Fondness to [her] Husband before any Witnesses?" Must Swift "hope" that this new bride will not be such a "fool" as to "still dream of Charms and Raptures; which Marriage ever did, and ever will put a sudden end to"? What sort of a friendly letter of welcome is this!

Well, it is, just the same, a friendly letter. We must understand that some of the harshest and shrewdest barbs are aimed not at Deborah Staunton but quite impersonally at "the generality of your Sex." It is they who employ "more Thought, Memory, and Application to be Fools, than would serve to make them wise." They are the ones who would worry their husbands into buying a new equipage instead of paying the butcher's bill; it is this "Knot of Ladies, got together by themselves," to chitchat "about a new Cargo of Fans" rather than attend to and take part in intelligent conversation with the entire company— it is *they* who are a "very School of Impertinence and Detraction." Such trivial people, men and women alike, are alas apt always to be part of our scene.

Furthermore, the letter is written in the straightforward terms of one reasonable person appealing to the good sense of another equally reasonable person. For the great Dean of St. Patrick's to write in such terms must have been flattering to this young woman. Finally, and of most importance, we have to meet head-on the criticism suggested previously, and neatly epitomized by so early a commentator as Mrs. Pilkington (Deborah Staunton "did not take [the Letter] as a compliment, either to her or the sex"[29]), and in this century by Temple Scott ("There is so little reverence for the individual addressed . . . that one can hardly wonder the precepts of so stern a Mentor were received by the Lady to whom they were addressed with more pique than complaisance"[30]).

If this *Letter* is read aright, Mrs. Pilkington and Temple Scott are wrong. I would say that a right reading begins with the knowledge that Swift's posture is from the first sentence ironical, and that Deborah Staunton and the Rochforts were aware of this. After the personal address of "Madam," Swift wrote: "The Hurry and *Impertinence* of receiving and paying Visits on Account of your Marriage, being now over; you are beginning to enter into a Course of Life, where you will want much Advice to divert you from falling into many *Errors, Fopperies,* and *Follies* to *which your Sex is subject*" (my italics). *Impertinence,* so egregiously the wrong word (but so right, too), signals at once the author's ironical stance. Immediately following is the reference to the "Errors, Fopperies, and Follies to which your sex is subject." Swift had been barking at females for years. Could Deborah not have known this?

I think it is fairly obvious that here Swift was playing, again, his game of tease-and-jab. In these first sentences he is teasing, and the rest of the short, first paragraph sustains this posture. He speaks of the groom ("my particular Favorite"); of his long-cherished hope that Deborah might make herself "worthy of him" (!); and of the lamentable fact that her parents had "failed" to "cultivate [Deborah's] mind." Finally, this great and formidable dean announces that he will be her director "as long as I shall think you deserve it, by letting you know how to act, and what you ought to avoid." I do not mean to allow the conclusion that Swift's rhetorical stance in this letter is all this sort of tease. A fair share of jabs are there, too, as we have seen. But even the sharpest of them ("You have but a few Years to be young and handsome in the Eyes of the World; and as few Months to be so in the Eyes of a Husband, who is not a Fool") are enveloped in a tone of affectionate irony that should not have given offense—at least not for long. Deborah probably did not faint in terror when she read this letter. I do not know what her reaction was. I suspect she read it thoughtfully and often smiled as she read.

Swift liked the role of tutor to a young lady—witness his relationships with Stella and Vanessa. It is interesting to see him again play that role and do so with the healthy conviction that a young lady had to *work* at making a success of her marriage, with the characteristically bleak conviction that the young lady who marries had best forget about love, but with the teasing and kindly authority of a wise and avuncular old friend.

Two phrases in the *Letter* direct us to *Gulliver's Travels*. To be sure, "le mythe animal" is present in much of Swift's writing,[31] but the particular application of that metaphor in this letter is directly suggestive of *Gulliver's Travels*. The relevant passage finds Swift saying that, when he reflects on the foolish behavior of females, he "cannot conceive [them] to be human Creatures, but a Sort of Species hardly a Degree above a Monkey; who hath more diverting tricks than any of [them]; [and] is an Animal less mischievous and expensive." In another passage, Swift writes that English ladies ought to relish discourse about "Travels into remote Nations"—a clear intimation of a text to be published in three years and on which he was even now working: *Travels into Several Remote Nations . . .* , by Lemuel Gulliver.

A Modest Proposal

A Modest Proposal is the most brilliant of a long series of Irish tracts by Swift. Ireland first learned about the *Proposal* in an advertisement in

the Dublin *Intelligence* for 8 November 1729: "The late apparent spirit
of patriotism, or love to our country, so abounding of late, has produced a new scheme, said in public to be written by D--S--, wherein
the author . . . ingenuously advises that one fourth part of the infants
under two years old, be forthwith fattened, brought to market and sold
for food, reasoning that they will be dainty bits for landlords, who as
they have already devoured most of the parents, seem to have the best
right to eat up the children."[32]

The character who "writes" the *Modest Proposal* is one, like Gulliver
and the hack writer of the *Tale* volume, that Swift will condemn for
moral obtuseness. The "modest" fellow who presents the *Proposal* invites our confidence (as Gulliver does), by a conversational and polite
tone and by an appearance of common sense and objectivity, only to
betray it (as does Gulliver also). More specifically, the narrator poses as
an economic "projector." His proposed "project" belongs to a well-
defined genre popular in Swift's day. For example, just a year earlier
(1728) the tireless Daniel Defoe had published his *Augusta Triumphans:
Or, the Way to Make London the most Flourishing City in the Universe,* a
publication that is a veritable portfolio of projects. It includes, among
others, "A proposal to prevent murder . . . ," "A proposal to prevent
the expensive importation of foreign musicians . . . ," and a proposal
to save "youths" and "servants" by clearing the streets of "shameless and
impudent strumpets." As an *economic* projector, Swift's narrator belongs
to the group of economic theorists of Swift's or any day who are either
innately or perversely blind, perhaps in the name of religion or science,
to the fact that people are neither animals, nor things, nor numbers. As
Martin Price says, "the Modest Proposer is not only a typical projector
but, more important, . . . [a] political arithmetician."[33] People are
seen as numbers, and it is only with numbers, therefore, that our
projector works.

In 1720 Swift had written to his friend Charles Ford: "I believe my
self not guilty of too much veneration for the Irish [House of Lords],
but I differ from you in Politicks [;] the Question is whether People
ought to be Slaves or no."[34] Swift's unhappiness at England's unjust
treatment of Ireland and the Irish people's own shameless and continuing willingness to be slaves was by no means new in 1729, when *A
Modest Proposal* appeared, or in 1720, when he made his comment to
Ford. In early years, the irritation was directed largely against the
English. As early as 1707 this concern had found expression in his *Story
of the Injured Lady,* an allegory of sorts in which the "Injured Lady" was

Ireland, and the injurer was England. Over the years that followed, however, Swift came to see that the victims (the Irish) in this sad drama were also the villains. At this point one distinguished critic sees another example in Swift's works of *le mythe animal* as expressing, according to Oliver Ferguson, "a point of view integral to Swift's judgment of Ireland. Swift is saying to the Irish, in effect, 'You have acted like beasts; hence you no longer deserve the title of men.' "[35]

With now two targets, the British and the Irish, Swift began in 1720 with his strongest onslaught on the terrible predicament his people were in. First came *The Proposal for the Universal Use of Irish Manufacture* (1720); the onslaught continued with the notorious *Drapier Letters* (1724–25); it was sustained by *A Short View of Ireland* (1727); and, though the attack did not cease in 1729, it reached its artistic culmination in that year with the publication of *A Modest Proposal,* one of the finest pieces of sustained irony in our language.

For this great series of Irish tracts, Swift earned his fame as patriot. He "received a silver box and the freedom of the City of Cork," Louis Landa tells us. "It was the Dean of St. Patrick's," he goes on to say, "who was gazed on affectionately as he walked through the alleys and streets of his Liberty. . . . It was the Anglican churchman who lived in easy intercourse with the great, the Lord Lieutenants and other statesmen, and whose literary genius was the admiration of friend and enemy alike."[36]

Ironically, it must be remembered that when Swift fought for Ireland and its beleaguered but undeserving people against England, he had most in mind a small percentage of the total population, the Anglo-Irish who belonged to the Established Church.[37] The Anglo-Irish Presbyterians were anathema, as were all "fanatics"; and the native Catholic Irish never did count very much at all in his calculations.

A good introduction to *A Modest Proposal* is Swift's *Short View of the State of Ireland,* published in 1727. It is an uncomplicated performance, presented by a nonironic persona (somewhat like the narrator in a *Letter to a Young Gentleman*) who in about half a dozen pages methodically presents the facts that later kindled the terrible satire of the *Proposal.* According to the *Short View,* the wretched and miserable state of Ireland was due to the fact that "[It] is the only Kingdom I ever heard or read of, either in ancient or modern Story, which was denied the Liberty of exporting their native Commodities and Manufactures. . . ."[38] Moreover, "One third Part of the Rents of Ireland, is spent in England . . . ," and "The Rise of our Rents is squeezed out of the very Blood, and Vitals, and Cloathes,

and Swellings of the Tenants; who live worse than English Beggars."
Also, "Both sexes [in Ireland], but especially the Women, despise and
abhor to wear any of their own Manufactures, even those which are better
made than in other countries. . . ."

Other facts were the dreadful Irish famines of the preceding three
years,[39] to which Swift does not refer explicitly, probably because they
were on so many men's minds anyway. One pamphlet of 1729 told of
people wandering about, searching desperately for food: "If they happen to hear of the death of a horse, they run to it as to a feast."[40] We
learn additional "facts" from M. B. Drapier's *Letter to the Whole People of
Ireland* (1724), in which Swift caused his persona (the Drapier) to
declare to the Irish: "By the Laws of God, of NATURE, of NATIONS,
and of your Country, you ARE and OUGHT to be as FREE a People as
your Brethren in England. . . . The Remedy is wholly in your own
Hands. . . ."[41]

In view of the sort of information listed above, the narrator of *A
Modest Proposal* is entirely in character as a reasonable man when he
suggests that Irish babies be butchered and sold for meat. In so terrible
a situation, what else could be done? The narrator believed (as did Swift
himself) that people were a nation's wealth. Babies are people. So sell
them. He is also "reasonable" when he proposes a thrifty consequence of
the slaughter: the babies' skins "will make admirable gloves for ladies,
and summer boots for fine gentlemen." As he methodically proceeds
("There is likewise another great Advantage in my Scheme") to tote up
his sums ("of the Hundred and Twenty Thousand Children, already
computed, Twenty thousand may be reserved for Breed"), Swift's de-
murrals are perfectly distinct: these are not advantages; this is not a
modest proposal; however disagreeable the child may be, she must not
be considered an animal 'reserved for Breed.' "

An arithmetical projector who believes that he has found a "fair,
cheap and easy method of making . . . children sound and useful members of the commonwealth" ought to be listened to. The situation of
Ireland was so bad that almost anybody who said he could improve
matters would get a hearing. This particular projector was guaranteed a
hearing because he had the persuasive qualities of objectivity, knowl-
edgeability, and an engaging modesty. It would seem, in truth, that
the distressing situation in Ireland could only be cured if fellow citizens
would imitate the "Modest Proposer," for there is no doubt that this
man's method and his attitude toward the problem were right. "Come,
let us reason together" was the appeal. Who could resist?

The trouble was not the method or the attitude, but the monster who employed them. Blind to human misery, he was incapable of realizing that people are not animals, or things, or numbers. He was a terrifyingly dangerous sort of person precisely because he *was* so objective, so knowledgeable, so modest, so limited, and so perfectly convinced that his conclusion was the best one thus far proposed. He insists, "I am not so violently bent upon my own Opinion, as to reject any offer . . . which shall be found equally innocent, cheap, easy, and effectual." And he concludes: "I have not the least personal Interest, in endeavouring to promote this necessary Work . . . I have no Children, by which I can propose to get a single Penny; the youngest being nine Years Old and my Wife past Child-bearing."

Most immediately, *The Modest Proposal* was Swift's contribution to the human predicament in Ireland in 1729. I agree with Edward W. Rosenheim's valuable discovery that, originally, the essay was intended primarily to voice Swift's monumental anger against the ruling class in Ireland for enduring with such spineless stupidity a situation that it was in their own power to cure, and that this reading does give to the *Proposal* a unity that other readings lack.[42] But I do not suppose that Professor Rosenheim would believe that isolating the contemporary "satiric target" necessarily explains the tremendous impact of the *Proposal* today. It will, to be sure, be long remembered in our language as a superb example of sustained irony, but more fundamental than a recognition of the rhetoric is the fact that people become upset and angry when they read this essay. The narrator is a monster: he has no right to talk about people as "breeders"; about babies, as meat. Thus by indirection is established the thesis most relevant to our times, and the main reason for its power among us. That this reason is not the primary one Swift intended is interesting but not terribly important. Neither did the architect intend his tower at Pisa to be remembered because it leans. Swift's *A Modest Proposal* is unforgettable not just as an indictment of the stupid and spineless Irish and of the British who took advantage of them; it is, I believe, unforgettable mainly as a warning. It warns that the very worst way to solve the problem of human misery is to give it to some modest-seeming, smooth-talking, thing-oriented political arithmetician and plug our ears when the screams begin.

Chapter Six
Gulliver's Travels

Gulliver's Travels was published in 1726, though the idea of the book had probably been conceived some time earlier. As early as 1711, in his *A New Journey to Paris,* Swift had created a character somewhat suggestive of Gulliver. The character is a traveler by the name of Sieur du Baudrier, who, as servant to Matthew Prior, pretended to report on the latter's negotiations, in Paris, to help the Tory ministry to end the War of the Spanish Succession. The Sieur du Baudrier's sober and "factual" account, purportedly "translated" into English, effectively served Swift's and the Tory party's intention of putting a favorable front on Prior's visit.[1] Another precursor of Gulliver was for many years thought to have been "born" in 1714, during the meetings of the Scriblerus Club. The club's assemblage of Tory geniuses—Pope, Parnell, Arbuthnot, Gay, and Swift—conceived the idea of a combined satiric project, the purpose of which Alexander Pope later described as being to ridicule "all the false tastes in learning, under the character of a man of capacity enough, that has dipped into every art and science, but injudiciously in each."[2] The central character of this project was apparently at one time intended to travel to some foreign lands. The prospectus thus vaguely suggests the possibility of a Gulliver being thought about. However, since Swift began work on the *Travels* early in 1721, Gulliver probably took final form much nearer to that date than to 1714, when the Scriblerus Club was holding its meetings. Ehrenpreis writes that "There is only a grain of truth in the old view that the book had its origins in the Scriblerus Club."[3] The "grain of truth" is perhaps enough, however, to allow the possibility that Swift's conversations in the Scriblerus Club and his writing, somewhat earlier, about Sieur de Baudrier were at least subliminally in mind when he began his writing in 1721. But, since facts are lacking, where Swift got his idea and precisely when he first consciously settled in his mind on the attributes of the character that eventually became Gulliver are questions that probably will never be settled.

In any event, Gulliver as metaphor is a very familiar figure and he has been around a very long time indeed. He is the loyal native who travels to a remote nation (or nations) and is sooner or later obliged to make a comparative evaluation of what he sees. Nobody has ever been sole proprietor of this device. For example, Plato, Lucian, and More had used it long before Swift, who was familiar with the works of all these men.[4] One of the more recent evidences, closer to our own day, appeared in 1960 in Lawrence Durrell's *Clea,* wherein is recorded the account of "A team of Chinese anthropologists [who] arrived in Europe to study our habits and beliefs. Within three weeks they were all dead. They died of uncontrollable laughter. . . ."

Swift was to employ his traveler as his narrator and was to use him, as he had used his other fictive narrators, as more or less of a mask behind or through which he would speak. Gulliver will be "more or less" of a mask because sometimes the mask will slip off, just as it did in the *Tale* volume, and we will hear Swift himself speaking out passionately and directly to us, perhaps sparked to the raw by some personal experience, suggested by the scene he is describing, that his outrageous pride refused to allow him to recollect with tranquility. But as a rule, the rhetorical posture in the *Travels* will be ironical and therefore Swift's voice will be different from Gulliver's.

Happily, in Swift's letters to Charles Ford facts are available about the dates and the chronology involved in the composition of the *Travels:* they indicate that he was busy writing his book in 1721; that, before the close of 1723, he had completed his account of Gulliver's first two voyages; that he finished the fourth voyage by January, 1724; that he then began the third voyage but, because of the interruption caused by his writing of *The Drapier Letters,* did not finish it until the middle of 1725.[5] In the following year *Gulliver's Travels* was published and, thanks to Alexander Pope's "prudent management" of the book's printing, it can be said that Swift's greatest book made him some money. Otherwise, he said, "I never got a farthing by anything I writ. . . ."[6]

Reactions to Gulliver's "Sting"

Gulliver's Travels meets two simple working definitions of a classic: it speaks powerfully and significantly to each generation; it never yields its full meaning. Any rereading is a new experience. Probably an exact rereading is in fact impossible since every reading is apt to yield revelations that turn the book into a different one—though not always or necessarily a better one.

For some readers, *Gulliver's Travels* lacks one attribute possibly not essential to, but at any rate possessed by, some of our greatest books: it is too negative; it offers no solution to the problem that it defines. Thus, if the book is taken as a revelation of the evil that in us lies, it gives no vision that encompasses the evil and, without palliating it, makes it at least for a moment bearable and perhaps somehow even understandable. Yet, despite this one reservation, testimony is well-nigh universal that *Gulliver's Travels* is one of the great books of the world.

Perhaps Swift's most famous comment about his book is the one he wrote to Pope in 1725: "The chief end I propose to my self in all my labors is to vex the world rather than divert it."[7] He was therefore distressed when Benjamin Motte, the London publisher, made some unauthorized changes in the 1726 (first) edition. These alterations were corrected in the 1735 Faulkner edition, but meanwhile Swift had complained dourly to Ford, "The whole Sting is taken out in several passages, in order to soften them. Thus the Style is debased, the humor quite lost, and the matter insipid."[8] The readers of Swift's day did not agree that "the humor [was] quite lost, and the matter insipid." Nor were they noticeably vexed. The reaction of his friends is typified by a letter from John Arbuthnot: "Gulliver is a happy man that at his age can write such a merry work."[9] John Gay wrote Swift a letter that indicates what an immediate and overwhelming success the book was with the general reading public: "About ten days ago a book was published here of the travels of one Gulliver, which has been the conversation of the whole town ever since: the whole impression sold in a week. . . . From the highest to the lowest it is universally read, from the Cabinet-council to the Nursery."[10]

The popular acclaim that Gay referred to is typical of the response accorded *Gulliver's Travels* in the early years of its publication. Although the interesting history of critical reaction thereafter is not properly the subject of this book,[11] I can note briefly that the merry enthusiasm of most of Gulliver's first readers did not last very long. Samuel Johnson, in his *Life of Swift* (1781), gives a fair summation of middle and late eighteenth-century opinion: "Criticism [of *Gulliver's Travels*] was for a while lost in wonder . . . But when distinctions came to be made the part which gave least pleasure was that which describes the Flying Islands [book 3], and that which gave most disgust must be the history of the Houyhnhnms [book 4]."[12] During the nineteenth century, criticism was generally condemnatory. It is perhaps not too much to say that most nineteenth-century critics felt some of Swift's stings, imagined some others, and strongly resented them all. A case in point is the comment made by William Thackeray in his *English Humourists of the Eighteenth Century* (published in 1853): looking upon the moral of the *Travels,* Thackeray said he thought it was "horrible, shameful, unmanly, blasphemous; and giant and great as this Dean is, I say we should hoot him." Leslie Stephen felt that book 4 was a "ghastly caricature," "lamentable and painful."[13]

Modern criticism is calmer, unsentimental, and probably better informed than any that precedes it. One reason is that in our day an impressive amount of research has revealed so much about the mind, art, and times of Dr. Swift; also, modern criticism has been most helpfully perceptive, particularly with respect to books 3 and 4. Finally, and doubtless also a factor, this century's appreciation of Swift has been increased because the threat of disaster is so often so close to us that readers more readily accept Swift's austere and gloomy visions. The critical history of *Gulliver's Travels* therefore indicates that its author was just about right in his remark: "The world glutted it self with that book at first, and now it will go off but soberly, but I suppose will not be soon worn out."[14]

Various Ways of Reading the Book

There are many ways to read *Gulliver's Travels*. A few ways, here referred to in general terms, will be explored later in more detail. First, then, *Gulliver's Travels* is a satire on travel books and on those, like Gulliver, who write them—or show their equivalent in our day on endless sequences of slides. Such people do not always sort out the trivial from the important experience: they show and tell far too much of some things and not enough of others. *Gulliver's Travels* is a story, too—often a very funny one (though it is not a novel). It is also topical satire on people and events of the day. In addition, because an author inevitably informs his work with his own mind and personality, *Gulliver's Travels* can be read in part and incidentally as a depiction of Swift himself. Probably some readers do read the book primarily in this fashion; but such an approach, legitimate for autobiography, limits a great imaginative prose satire and is likely to give a distorted picture of the man. Moreover, especially in our times, Gulliver may at the end be regarded as one of those tragic and alienated eccentrics hopelessly traumatized by and unable to come to a sensible reading of what life has dealt him.

Gullliver's Travels is allegory, wherein two satiric butts are gradually discovered.[15] One of the emerging targets is Gulliver himself, for his naiveté, for his misrepresentations of facts, and for his absurd illusions when, at the end, he sinks deeply into misanthropy; the other satiric butt is humankind generally, for its pride, its treacheries and betrayals, its dirtiness, and for its perverse refusal to look long enough and accurately enough at the surface of things so that, seeing beneath, it may learn the difference between the shell and the kernel (even though the kernel may be rotten, too!), between truth and falsehood, between good and evil. Many of these ways of reading *Gulliver's Travels* will be touched on in the pages that follow, though for most readers probably the allegorical reading will finally dominate. However, their interpretations of the allegory, and their reactions to it, will vary widely.

The wonderful variety of interpretations is suggested to us by James Clifford in a fine summary-statement of what he calls the "basic approaches" to the ending of *Gulliver's Travels*. The comments are intended to apply most specifically to book 4, the ending, but in truth they are relevant in some ways to the whole of *Gulliver's Travels*. According to Professor Clifford, readers' reactions divide generally into two groups: those who prefer the "hard" approach, and those who prefer the "soft" approach. "By 'hard,' " Clifford has written, "I mean an interpretation which stresses the shock and difficulty of the work, with almost tragic overtones, while by 'soft' I mean the tendency to find comic passages and compromise solutions."[16] A formidable list of distinguished scholars may be found on each side of this probably never-to-be-settled question.[17]

Finally, Clifford suggests that, depending upon the approach taken, a reader at the end of *Gulliver's Travels* may feel that he has read a tragic, a shocking, a comic, a satiric, or perhaps even a didactic work.[18] This is no doubt true for some readers. I believe, however, that all of these approaches apply to my discussion. I would therefore prefer to say that no single one of them, alone, seems to me to describe *Gulliver's Travels* satisfactorily. Thus not only book 4 of the *Travels* but at various times and in varying degrees all of Swift's writings can be described as tragic, shocking, comic, satiric, or didactic. Because of my eclectic approach to Swift's works, and because I do find "comic passages" and "compromise solutions" to book 4 of the *Travels,* Clifford would place me among those who prefer the "soft" approach.

A Voyage to Lilliput (Book 1)

The first impression this book leaves on the reader is usually that of verisimilitude. Facing the beginning of the first chapter is a map, and it looks accurate and real: but it is in fact neither. Swift begins in the same fashion each of the accounts of Gulliver's four voyages; it is one of the many recurring devices in his book. He also includes pictorial representations of various sorts; and, as a letter to his publisher reveals, he thought them important because they undeniably gave the appearance of truth-telling to his account.[19]

The early pages of *Gulliver's Travels* demands an unusually attentive reading. For example, on the very first page are those carefully chosen details that suggest accurate and honest reporting. Gulliver spent "three years" at "Emanuel-College in Cambridge"; he "studied Physick" at Leyden for "two years and seven Months"; he "married Mrs. Mary Burton, second Daughter to Mr. Edmund Burton." These and other details dispose us to suspend immediately any possibility of disbelief about this obviously true tale of a voyage of this undoubtedly honest man.

The first sentence of this first page reads, "My Father had a small estate in Nottinghamshire; I was the third of five sons." The "I" is of course Gulliver, the presumed narrator behind and through whom Swift will speak. It is as usual important to realize immediately something of what this narrator—Lemuel Gulliver—is, and is not. The "small estate" in Nottinghamshire makes him a member of the middle class living in the middle of England. As "the third of five sons" he is also a middle son. Though the repetition of "middle" was perhaps not intentional and certainly proves nothing, it may be taken as suggestive: Gulliver is a middling sort of person, a sort of Mr. Average: one of us.[20]

As with some of his poetry, the first page of Swift's *Travels* raises the problem of this author's coprophilia. Traditionally, some readers have always felt offended by Swift's spending so much time, as they thought, fluttering in and around muck and feces. Traditionally, too, young people who read *Gulliver's Travels* were likely to read a text from which passages thought by censors to be offensive were expurgated. Predictably, the psychoanalysts have found Swift a rich and irresistible vein to explore. The *Psychoanalytic Review* of 1942 offers an instance of this approach. As there explained, *Gulliver's Travels* presents "abundant evidence of the neurotic makeup of the author and discloses in him a number of perverse trends indicative of fixation at the anal sadistic state of libidinal development. Most conspicuous among those perverse trends is that of coprophilia, although the work furnishes evidence of numerous other related neurotic characteristics accompanying the general picture of psychosexual infantilism and emotional immaturity."[21] Earnest research by a psychoanalytical critic has also recently resulted in a report that Virginia Woolf's many problems can be explained by the news that her mother terminated breast-feeding her at too early an age (*Virginia Woolf Miscellany,* 1987).

It may be that there are other explanations for Swift's and Woolf's adult behavior. In Swift's case it seems to me that some of the so-called scatology can be sensibly enough explained in terms of his era and of its literary traditions, to which he was always sensitive. Thus Irvin Ehrenpreis concludes in an enlightened chapter (published in 1953) on Swift's "obscenity": "Swift's writing is sometimes coarse or bawdy. . . . If we are shocked, let us admit it is traditions that shock us, not the man."[22] As Ehrenpreis demonstrates, a lot of what we might call coarse and bawdy today was not thought to be so by Swift's contemporaries. Obviously traditions have changed, and it is the traditions of Swift's own time that we have to know about in order to make any sense out of his comment— made about his poetry but applicable I believe also to his prose—that he wrote "never any {work} without a moral View."[23]

Two other ways of looking at this vexing problem might be mentioned. One is that a thoughtful reader might consider the possibility that the scatology or coprophilia really serves some functional purpose in the work being considered. The other possibility is simply that Swift was having fun. Both these possibilities are applicable to the wordplay on the first page of *Gulliver's Travels,* where he sports coyly with *Mr. James Bates.* James Bates becomes successively *Mr. Bates;* then *my good master, Mr. Bates;* then *Mr. Bates my master;* and finally, at the bottom of the page, since there was not much sense in teetering on the edge of this sorry joke any longer, *my good master Bates.*[24] An ancient tradition, including such figures in the history of English literature as Chaucer and Shakespeare, would surely permit Swift to have this sort of locker-room fun. But a reader should also note that this passage may be seen as serving a functional purpose since it can be read as Swift's early admonishment to "Be sure to read with care, and you'll find some very odd things here."[25]

Very early in book 1 a major recurring device appears that helps to unify both structurally and thematically the whole of the *Travels.* This device is the accident that precipitates Gulliver into the central action of each book. In book 1 it is a shipwreck. Actually, nobody could be very much blamed for this first accident. But by book 4 the event that puts Gulliver into Houyhnhnmland is a betrayal by his own shipmates. Here there is blame. Thus Arthur Case's remarks: "The accidents by which Gulliver arrives in the several countries which he visits are varied not only for the sake of novelty, but to keep pace with his growing realization of the defects of human nature."[26] The reader does well to look for this and other devices that give structural and thematic unity to the book.

The early pages of book 1 present the little people (the six-inch tall Lilliputians) and the "little language" that appears throughout the *Travels*. These little people of book 1 reveal themselves to be as small morally as they are physically. The recognition of their pettiness comes gradually to the reader, and the moment of realization will no doubt vary from reader to reader, depending on such factors as his alertness, his temperament, and his experience with irony. The timing of the moment is unimportant, however, just so long as he discovers somewhere along the line that the hosts on this voyage are something other than merely engaging and cuddly. They gossip meanly about each other; they fight over such trivial matters as which end of an egg should be broken first; and their king is angry when Gulliver refuses to help him bring a neighboring country into slavery.

About the language of these tiny folk, and of the residents of other lands that Gulliver visits, critics have exercised considerable ingenuity, though their attempts at translation made thus far do not seem to me to enrich markedly our reading of this text. There are a few suggestions that are generally accepted, however. In Book 4, the language is clearly intended to sound like the talk of horses—if horses could talk. The words of the "little language" are obviously a verisimilar device, and they do occasionally have special meanings: *Gulliver* is gullible; *Tribnia* and *Langden* are anagrams for "Britain" and "England"; *hurgo* is perhaps a rogue. But beyond this, most of the words and names must be read as the untranslatable language of some never-never land. Further exploration of the problems now almost invites Mark Twain's words: "the researches of many commentators have already thrown much darkness on this subject, and it is probable that, if they continue, we shall soon know nothing at all about it."

Also, early in the account of Gulliver's first voyage, we encounter one of the several instances in the *Travels* of satire on travel books and travelers, perhaps a vestige of Swift's association with the Scriblerus

Club. The first such instance occurs in chapter 2 when Gulliver "for some hours extremely pressed by the necessities of nature . . . was under great difficulties between urgency and shame." "The best expedient I could think on," he writes, "was to creep into my house, which I accordingly did; and shutting the gate after me, I went as far as the length of my Chain would suffer; and discharged my body of that uneasy load. . . . I cannot but hope the candid Reader will [not be offended], after he hath impartially considered my case, and the distress I was in." The scatological problem, discussed above, need not interfere with an understanding of what Swift, through Gulliver, is here satirizing: the ridiculous traveler who reports everything about his trip, even details about his bowel movements. Again in this instance, therefore, the scatology serves a functional purpose.

Finally, readers of the beginning pages of this book should be aware of what is called its "topical" satire. For instance, when Flimnap in book 1 maintains himself in office by doing tricks on a tightrope, Swift is satirizing a lively "topic" of the day: the political activities of Robert Walpole, the Whig prime minister of England. When the curious Lilliputian throngs are ordered "not to come within fifty yards of [Gulliver's] house, without licence from the court, whereby the secretaries of state got considerable fees," Swift is satirizing the bureaucratic thievery usually presumed to be more or less in the nature of things in London or in Dublin. Much later, in book 3, when Laputa fails to bring Balnibarbi under subjection, Swift is referring to Ireland's successful resistance to the introduction of Wood's halfpence.

But this topical aspect of *Gulliver's Travels* is customarily of little interest to a modern reader. In general, the book is read today not because it was appropriate and relevant to men and events in Swift's time, but because it meaningfully relates to people and events in our time. In the instances referred to above, therefore, the lesson for us is that oppression of any sort should be resisted, that an entrenched officialdom will inevitably exact bribes whenever possible, and that a people's leader should not win and maintain his position by spectacularly demonstrating skills that are irrelevant to what is needed. Great gymnastic skills are surely not the right criteria by which to measure a country's leaders.

Now, assuming that we have read not only these early pages but the whole of book 1, what major points stand out? First, we have learned to know and like the narrator. He seems to be a well-intentioned and likeable fellow, very quick at picking up a new language, whose narration appears to be so straightforward and so rich in convincing details that we do want to believe him. But even this early in the first of the four books we have to be careful. When Gulliver says (1:6), "I defy the Treasurer . . . to prove that any person ever came to me incognito," his comment should normally be taken to mean that he had no such visitors; actually, however, at the very beginning of the next chapter he betrays himself by telling about one occasion when a "considerable person . . . came to my house very privately at night." When Gulliver succeeded in putting out the fire at the queen's residence after three minutes of copiously urinating, we have no question that the fire was doused, but we might wonder about a person's ability to continue copious urination for three minutes. When Gulliver says that 500,000 Lilliputians live in the capital city of Mildano, a reader must note that Mildano is 500 feet square. That is the equivalent of a room twenty-five feet long and twenty feet wide. Five hundred thousand Lilliputians can get in there? Gulliver has got to be wrong in his figuring. When he soberly assures us that not a particle of scandal should be attached to the relationship between him and the wife of the lord treasurer, his elaborate defense skirts mention of the really significant consideration: he is six feet tall and she is six inches tall. Gulliver is sometimes not only inaccurate; sometimes he is also naive.

We know our narrator better if we are alert to the voices of irony in this unfolding narrative. In fact, as suggested above, a great part of our enjoyment comes from being on the lookout for, and discovering, these differing voices. In the reference just made to Gulliver's attempt to vindicate the reputation of a lady unjustly accused of an adulterous relationship with him, the surface meaning is of course Gulliver's. Swift's voice should also be heard, chuckling and saying something like, "Isn't Gulliver silly?" The same "other voice" is noted when Gulliver urinates on the apartment of her imperial majesty. He did flood the fire out, but he is perplexed when the empress conceived "the greatest abhorrence of what I had done" and removed to "the most distant side of the court." Why should the empress be offended by floods of urine on her apartment? Gulliver does not understand. Swift of course does. Again, when the emperor announces his "lenient" decision to blind Gulliver and then starve him to death, Gulliver is distressed. He concludes that the lowness of his birth and the deficiencies of his education prevent him from regarding the sentence as lenient. Swift's voice emerges clearly: one needs neither a high birth nor an extensive education to see so obvious a fact. One needs only to see a thing as it is. The "thing" in this instance is cruel, not "lenient." In such passages, Swift is judging Gulliver. He is not yet unrelentingly condemning, as he will be before he finishes with him in book 4; but he has already begun to insist that the words of this British sailor should be weighed very carefully. Like most people, Gulliver cannot see straight sometimes, and sometimes he does not see at all. He has glasses, to be sure, but he seldom puts them on.

Finally, if a major thesis sustained by book 1 is that Gulliver has the limitations of an average person, it is also true that the book shows him to be at least morally superior to the little people who are his hosts. For example, he does not have their small meannesses or pettiness. When the Lilliputian emperor tries to enlist Gulliver's help in subjugating the Blefuscudians, Gulliver protests: "I would never be an instrument of bringing a free and brave people into slavery" (1:5). Thus, measured by the moral norm that they provide, he, like any average man, has cause to be reasonably satisfied with himself. Also, like any average man who is satisfied with himself, his travels have thus far taught him very little, if anything.

A Voyage to Brobdingnag (Book 2)

In book 2 recur such structural or thematic devices as the map, the shipwreck that precipitates Gulliver into the central action of this voyage, and the usual attention given to specific detail. For example, Gulliver's first experience in this new land is to see, from a distance, a giant; then he comes upon grass twenty feet high, and corn forty feet high. Such verisimilar details speedily transport us to the book's usual paradox: belief in a make-believe land that does exist.

Gulliver, just recently big in a land of little people, is now little in a land of giants. It is perhaps too much to say that a reader is thus prepared to expect that Gulliver will not fare very well judged by the moral norms of big people. But that in fact is what happens for, his host decides, little Gulliver belongs to a race of "little odious vermin." Nonetheless, for his readers Gulliver yet has saving graces. He is still a fascinating reporter; he has a wonderful loyalty to his country; he is resourceful; he is well-intentioned. To be sure occasionally he again appears somewhat ridiculous: he has to swim for his life when thrown into a pitcher of cream; he rows in his large boat, which would hold eight humans (but "when I had done . . . Glumdalclitch [his little forty-foot-tall nurse] hung it up to dry"); he takes a flying leap that lands him in the middle of a cow dung (Swift does not give us the dimensions of the Brobdingnagian cows, but we can guess that the cow dung is about three feet deep and five to six feet wide); Gulliver plays a jig on his host's spinet by running up and down a sixty-foot platform, banging away at the keys ("the most violent exercise I ever underwent"). But these activities do not seriously diminish our affection for him; instead, they illustrate once again the fact that *Gulliver's Travels* has in it a great deal of quite uncomplicated fun.

A more sober reaction to book 2 develops when, on the one hand, we study what Gulliver observes and says about the Brobdingnagians and, on the other, when we hear his chief host, the Brobdingnagian king, calmly and objectively add up the meaning of all the facts that the little visitor has given him about "civilized" life in England.

A major structural device of the *Travels* is confrontation: in each of the four books, Gulliver confronts a culture different from his own, engages in conversation with a superior, most notably with the emperor (book 1), with the king (book 2) and with his master (book 4), and is examined by his hosts for information about his homeland. Implicit in these confrontations is the expectation that, after pondering the evidence each side learns from the other, honest comparisons will be made among the various cultures. Such a comparison was made by Montaigne, an author with whom Swift was familiar, in his essay "Of Cannibals." In an astonishingly objective study Montaigne concluded that the culture of the cannibals was in most respects distinctly superior to that of "civilized" Europe. But Gulliver is not yet ready in book 2 to make the admission that anything foreign could possibly be better than what he had at home.

Three or four instances illustrate the workings of the confrontation device in book 2. In the first of these, when Gulliver is on a shopping trip with his nursemaid and friend, Glumdalclitch, beggars crowd around the coach he is in. He sees a woman with a cancerous breast "full of holes, in two or three of which I could have easily crept." This sight is bad enough, but what most distresses him was the lice of these people. He can see "their snouts with which they rooted like swine." Swift's implication is all too clear: whatever Gulliver (man) can see on and in the skin of a giant Brobdingnagian, microscopic eyes can see on Gulliver (and man). It is a vulgar and humbling notion: lice, "rooting like swine," are in the folds of fat in every man's belly—but not yet, for he does not see them, in Gulliver's—nor probably not yet the reader, in his.

In one memorable passage in book 2, Gulliver, like the narrator in "A Beautiful Young Nymph Going to Bed," becomes the envy of all our vulgar crowd of Peeping Toms. Gulliver is brought right into the apartments of the maids of honor, where, of course, he is still the invisible peeper, for the young ladies regard him not as a man but as a kind of toy. He watches them dress and undress. They do not hesitate in his presence "to discharge what they had drunk, to the quantity of at least two hogs heads." (As ladies, incidentally, these young women are also invisible to Gulliver. Like Swift himself, insisting that we see the physical grossness of the body and of bodily functions, he is filled with emotions of "horror and disgust.") The voice of Swift, behind Gulliver, is again saying: "Look at yourself, especially if you are a female, and most especially if you think yourself lovely; excepting for your size, in what way are you less vulgar than these Brobdingnagians?"

One interesting feature of this boudoir scene is that the redoubtable Gulliver faints for the first time. He can endure being placed upon the bare bosom of one of these maids of honor, for the natural smell of sixty feet of Brobdingnagian female is bearable, he discovers, though not pleasant. However, if the maid is perfumed, Gulliver "immediately swooned away." That a gigantic physical stimulus (the stench of a perfumed female Brobdingnagian) should cause Gulliver to faint is entirely reasonable. Moreover, if and when Gulliver learns the major lesson of his voyages—when he learns to assess and evaluate his experience—he will react consistently and just as emphatically to what Swift would regard as more important: a moral "smell" will cause him to faint.

But Gulliver's moral sensitivity is at this point elementary. The moral heights to which his hosts in book 2 reach simply baffle him, a fact clearly demonstrated when our ingenuous little traveler gives his host an "exact account of the government of England," and his majesty in Brobdingnag draws a line under the evidence and states the obvious conclusion: "My little friend Grildrig," for that is what they called him, "you have made a most admirable panegyric upon your country. You have clearly proved that ignorance, idleness, and vice, are the proper ingredients for qualifying a legislator. That laws are best explained, interpreted, and applied by those whose interests and abilities lie in perverting, confounding, and eluding them. I observe among you some lines of an institution, which in its original might have been tolerable; but these half erased, and the rest wholly blurred and blotted by corruptions . . ." Therefore, by "what I [the Brobdingnagian king] have gathered from your own relation, and the answers I have with much pains wringed and extorted from you, I cannot but conclude the bulk of your natives to be the most pernicious race of little odious vermin that nature ever suffered to crawl upon the surface of the earth" (2:6). It is a devastating and memorable passage; also, as in the "Digression on Madness" in *The Tale of a Tub* and in much of book 4 of *Gulliver's Travels,* it is I think the voice of Jonathan Swift that we hear.

On the evidence that Gulliver gives, the indictment is as accurate as it is severe. To Gulliver at this stage, however, the indictment is merely an astonishing error. With a lovely condescension he explains that the king has lived "secluded from the rest of the world" and has therefore been victimized by obvious "prejudices" and "a certain narrowness of thinking." As a consequence Gulliver believes that, by performing what *he* considers a kind and generous act, the king will be forced to adopt a less severe and a more accurate opinion of mankind: he therefore generously offers the king the secret of gunpowder, explaining that with this weapon its owner can divide hundreds of enemy bodies in the middle, rip up pavements, dash out brains, and so on. The king is horrified at such "inhuman ideas." Gulliver's own moral blindness prevents him from any reaction other than honest bewilderment. He cannot understand why anybody should "let slip" so grand an opportunity.

So book 2 really ends with a series of questions. Gulliver has now confronted three civilizations: his own (and, roughly speaking, ours), the Lilliputians', the Brobdingnagians'. Does he compare, evaluate, or assess? Have his travels made any difference? He has looked at a vision of Utopia in the "original" institutions of the Lilliputians (chapter 6); he has seen a kind of Utopia in the land of the large-souled Brobdingnagians. Compared morally with these big "people," he clearly does not—and thus we do not, as Mr. Average—get off unscathed. But does Gulliver begin to think less of his own civilization or of himself? Does Gulliver think at all? Not much; not yet—but when he returns to civilization, he does experience some problems of physical maladjustment, for everything looks small to him: "I began to think of myself in Lilliput. I was afraid of trampling on every traveller I met, and often called aloud to have them stand out of the way. . . . When I came to my own house . . . one of the servants opening the door, I bent down to go in (like a goose under a gate) for fear of striking my head. My wife ran out to embrace me, but [she looked so small] I stooped lower than her knees." In other words, there are problems of physical adjustment for Gulliver, but there is as yet no sign of any moral adjustment. He has no real problems of that sort yet. They will come later.

A Voyage to Laputa, Balnibarbi, Glubdubdrib, Luggnagg, and Japan (Book 3)

As the letters to Ford reveal, Swift finished his "Voyage to the Houyhnhnms" (book 4 of *Gulliver's Travels*) and then commenced work on the "Voyage to Laputa, Balnibarbi, Luggnagg, Glubdubdrib, and Japan" (book 3). This accident of composition led George Sherburn to state: "These letters [to Ford] also make it apparent that the third voyage was the last to be written. The fourth, then, should be only hesitantly regarded as the final drawing of the curtain of gloom."[27] Although this comment is astute and relevant to a biography of Swift, what is important to us is that Swift himself placed the "Voyage to the Houyhnhnms" last. Book 3 must therefore be studied as book 3 because that is what it is. Book 4 must be regarded as book 4 and thus even, if you will, as "the final drawing of the curtain of gloom."

Book 3 is not generally so highly regarded as other sections of the *Travels*. "[T]he part which gave the least pleasure," wrote Samuel Johnson, "is that which describes the Flying Island. . . ."[28] The reasons are both obvious and, it seems to me, sufficient—though I should like, before finishing this discussion, to make a claim for the positive merit that this book has, and which distinguished scholars have most persuasively pointed out. But the story line of book 3, which includes the account of Gulliver's visit to the flying island of Laputa, will probably always be thought the weakest of all the four books. The construction, almost entirely episodic, consists of a series of anecdotes that develop only slight and momentary suspense, as in the account of the attempt to put down the rebellion in Lindalino. Narrative tension is nowhere long sustained. In addition, as with the *Tale* volume, the satire seems at times rather more sprayed than aimed. To be sure, there are some specific targets. Swift's continuing interest in history and in historiography explains one of these targets: those "prostitute" historians who do not report truly "The springs and motives of great enterprises and revolutions in the world, and of the contemptible accidents to which they owed their success."

Another specific target is the idea of immortality, as it is sentimentally and naively understood by Gulliver. In his references to the struldbrugs (chapter 10) we hear Swift's voice insisting that, since the forces of nature inexorably bring decay, it is better to die before these forces condemn the body to an old age that merely grows increasingly burdensome, disgusting, and horrible. The account implies gratitude that natural infirmities, which every second are helping us to rot and wither away, are allowed no more time than they already have. It is reason for thanksgiving that death normally wins the race against rot.

A third specific target illustrates some of the topical satire in this book. Like *The Drapier Letters,* one section (chapter 3 of book 3) satirizes the British attempt to introduce Wood's halfpence into Lindalino (Dublin). In a half dozen paragraphs, regarded by eighteenth-century publishers as too dangerous to print, but included in modern editions, Swift records the failure of the British "to reduce this proud people" of Ireland. Though this and other specific targets may be easily enough pointed out, book 3 does nonetheless lack the unity, as prose satire, of books 1, 2, and 4.[29] Rather, what readers will find in this book is a Swiftean congregation of grievances, with—as will be pointed out in a moment—one offense standing out above the rest. For most readers, therefore, book 3 will probably end up having a dominant, rather than a unifying, theme.

Lastly, an obvious failure of book 3 is Swift's unsuccessful manipulation of his narrator, Gulliver. Throughout these four voyages, an overwhelming question continues to be, "Will it ever occur to Gulliver, in his confrontation with the various cultures that he meets, to assess his own culture and himself and by implication the whole family of men and women, in the light of what he has seen and heard?" Perhaps the revelation of damaging fact after damaging fact may not affect Gulliver at all. This has been known to be the result quite often with your average man and woman. Perhaps the whole of the truth may strike Gulliver in a sudden terribly illuminating moment and the course of his life will be radically altered for the better. This, more rarely, has also happened. Or perhaps part of the truth may strike Gulliver (as it does, in book 4) and change his life in a less desirable but not less dramatic way than if he had seen all of the truth. In book 3 Swift never settled on any of these alternatives. Though his own attitude is clear about the various experiences he depicts, we do not always know what Gulliver is thinking. The reason is that, though Swift now and again makes an awkward shift to remind us that it is Gulliver who is relating this account ("I hope," reported Gulliver, "the reader need not be told that I do not in the least intend my own country in what I say upon this occasion" (3: 6), we do really hear his voice. In fact, we hardly think Gulliver is there. When we hear "I told [the host] that in the Kingdom of Tribnia [that is, Britain] . . . the bulk of the people consisted wholly of discoverers, witnesses, informers, accusers, prosecutors, evidences, swearers . . . ," the "I" actually seems to be the angry dean, Jonathan Swift himself.

Swift's mismanagement of Gulliver in book 3 has occasioned many interesting comments. Kathleen Williams, for example, writes that, "whether or not Swift planned it so, Gulliver's virtual lack of function, indeed of existence, in the 'Voyage to Laputa' has a certain effectiveness in contributing to the atmosphere of meaningless activity and self-deceit, leading to a shadowy despair."[30] But I think even more interesting are possibilities of speculation about the *end* of book 3. The fact of a recurring pattern of return in the other three voyages sets up a certain expectation; and, when this expectation is not fulfilled, the situation does most especially invite comment.

Instead of the quite detailed accounts in the other three voyages, Gulliver's return in book 3 is disposed of quite summarily. Specifically, in each of the other three voyages, Gulliver and the captain of the ship that brings him home talk at some length. A study of the meetings between Gulliver and these captains suggests that the latter's function in books 1 and 2, and as it will be again in book 4, is to assist Gulliver in his readjustment to "normal" humanity, where most of the people are pretty much his own kind and shape. At the end of book 3, however, the captain is barely mentioned. He has almost no conversation with Gulliver. Indeed, to secure passage aboard ship, Gulliver rejects his identity and poses as a Dutchman. Therefore, since in a sense he no longer exists, there can be no conversation between him and the captain. Perhaps this is also the reason why Gulliver has no problems of readjustment, physical or moral, at the end of the third voyage. The "real" Gulliver did not take the trip. This fact, in turn, intriguingly delivers to us an ironic twist of the familiar story of the mythic figure who loses his life, only to find it. The Gulliver who ceases to exist in book 3 is the Gulliver who is "born anew" in book 4.

No critic has yet proclaimed book 3 to be the best work Swift ever wrote. On the whole, as we have seen, it must still be considered a kind of satiric grab bag, with little narrative interest. But scholars and critics in our day, giving long-neglected book 3 a long look, have been so illuminating in their researches and comments that the book's merit shows forth clearly and to better effect than before.[31]

First, a more sympathetic reading of book 3 was made possible when one important misconception was removed: research proved that Swift, though he had no affection for it, was not ignorant of science:[32] he read the proceedings of the Royal Academy of Science. Also he and his Scriblerus Club friends had apparently some notion of the fact, long before *Gulliver's Travels* was written, that the problem was not science (or art) as such, but rather the superficial dilettante who "dipped into every art and science" and "injudiciously in each."[33] If Swift sometimes erred (as he did) in his judgment of what the scientists were doing, his errors are understandable. Who could have foreseen that sunshine (vitamin D) could indeed be extracted from cucumbers?[34] Who could have foreseen that, for the modern traveler in outer space, the disposition of human excrement would present a problem requiring highly skilled technicians?

Second, book 3 is given some moments of great power by its one most dominant theme, one that is illustrated when we read that the better class of Gulliver's hosts had need for a type of domestic called a flapper. The Laputan of consequence, so wonderfully adept at abstract thought, must be attended by a servant "employed diligently to attend his master in his walks, and upon occasion to give him a soft flap on his eyes, because he is always so wrapped up in cogitation, that he is in manifest danger of falling down every precipice, and bouncing his head against every post, and in the streets, of jostling others, or being jostled himself into the kennel" (3:2). Though to get an island to fly, as these Laputans did, is a feat of astounding theoretical and practical skill, it is a skill that Swift ignored. What did impress him was that, in all matters that as a satirist he was driven to observe, these abstract theorists lacked the most ordinary kind of common sense. They are funny, as a result (at least to us), but they were more than merely amusing to Swift. We do hear him laughing sardonically at such absurd projects as "softening marbles for pillows" and breeding "naked sheep." The laugh continues, somewhat more bitterly, with the discovery that, among these people, "a man born blind . . . was to mix colors." In the fields "even one ear of corn or a blade of grass" is rarely seen, so foolish and unproductive are the new agricultural policies (3:4). The results of such policies and activity were patently disastrous to the fabled residents of Lagado and by implication would be to any people comparably victimized by delusion. This satire of what seemed to Swift the senseless and obviously impractical abstractions of projectors and pseudoscientists is, I believe, the major theme of book 3.

Bonamy Dobrée has a very good comment about this satire. He writes: "Swift objected to the absurd pretensions of the second-rate scientists to explain the inexplicable: he objected to the self-glorification of the petty virtuoso dissecting flies." None of these activities were of any importance. Dobrée continues: "[Swift] was really asking the question, 'What is the proper object of man's most strenuous intellectual attention?' "[35] The question needed asking in 1726; it needs asking now. That book 3, despite its obvious limitations, forces this question into prominence is the best explanation of its worth.

A Voyage to the Country of the Houyhnhnms (Book 4)

Before the disastrous fourth voyage begins, Gulliver is obviously still very much the average man, perhaps shaken up a bit, but generally doing and thinking as average men usually do. On his way to his ship he leaves a pregnant wife behind him, just as many another sailor has through the ages. At any rate, Gulliver on this voyage is very speedily thrust into the central action with which book 4 is primarily concerned. His predicament this time is caused by the very worst sort of treachery: his own men betray him, their captain. Thus, as Arthur Case has said, "The accidents by which Gulliver arrives in the several countries . . . are varied . . . to keep pace with his growing realization of the defects of human nature."[36] In fact Gulliver is not quite ready to admit to these "defects," but the realization is now certainly very near.

The action of book 4 concerns Gulliver's life with the horses (Houyhnhnms) and the revolting, filthy, apelike figures (Yahoos). During his three years in the land ruled by these Houyhnhnms, Gulliver is so favorably impressed by his equine hosts that he wishes to live out his days among them. His wish reflects the fact that he has finally "awakened." He now compares; he assesses. The result is a thorough rejection of his own species and the civilization it has constructed. A major tension of the entire four books of Gulliver's Travels is thus resolved; but it is resolved very dramatically in terms that belong to the Houyhnhnm-Yahoo world.

The question is of course, "Is Gulliver a Yahoo?" If he is a Yahoo, then the species of which he is a fair representative is also filthy Yahoo and its culture is Yahoo. Gulliver knows he is not, protests that he is not, but is finally relentlessly driven to the fact that he is a Yahoo. The climactic scene comes about when he gets permission from the sorrel nag—who plays the guardian role in this book 4 that Glumdalclitch played in book 2—to wash in a river. As he strips himself naked and bathes, he is observed by a young female Yahoo. The unclothed Gulliver so teases the desires of this young female that, inflamed with passion, she assaults our hero. "I roared as loud as I could," reports Gulliver. The sorrel nag, galloping up, saves him from what novelists used to call "a fate worse than death." Gulliver's reaction to his near-rape is a sobering one: ". . . now I could no longer deny that I was a real Yahoo in every limb and feature, since the females had a natural propensity to me, as one of their own species." Most of book 4 is concerned with validating this equation: Gulliver = Yahoo. Our task is not at this point to test the truth of the equation; instead, it is to see how Swift gives support to his proposition. Particularly effective in this proof is the recurring device of the conversation between the traveler and his host. In this confrontation, Gulliver speaks of war ("a soldier is a Yahoo hired to kill in cold blood as many of his own species who have never offended him, as possibly he can"). Gulliver tells about lawyers "among us," whose purpose is to demonstrate that "white is black and black is white." He tells about doctors and how they kill off "husbands and wives grown weary of their mates." He speaks of the nobility, "bred from childhood in idleness and luxury." Now, as a matter of fact, Swift numbered among his friends many good and great men who were lawyers (for example, Robert Rochfort, Lord Chief Baron of the Court of the Exchequer in Ireland), doctors (John Arbuthnot was one), or nobles (Harley the Earl of Oxford; Henry St. John, Viscount Bolingbroke; and Baron Carteret, who was Lord Lieutenant of Ireland when Swift was writing his *Travels.*) It is clear, therefore, that Gulliver's report to his host exhibits Swift's familiar distortion device.

Just as in important parts of all books of the *Travels,* just as in many parts of the *Tale* volume (1704 and 1710) and in such poems as "A Beautiful Young Nymph Going to Bed" (1730), Swift's technique can be explained, though this explanation does not for a moment—at least for most readers—palliate its corrosive force. The technique is the result of a dour vision that instinctively and with great sureness searches out what seems to that vision the most significant fact or facts (ignoring all others) in any situation and then graphically depicts what it sees. As an instance, consider the Brobdingnagian nurse; she has only one distinguishing physical feature: a "monstrous breast, [whose] nipple was about half the bigness of my head, and the hue both of that and the dug so varified with spots, pimples and freckles, that nothing could appear more nauseous" (2:1). This sort of brutal caricature of the truth is perhaps what lies behind Hugo Reichard's shrewd observation that

"[Gulliver] provides unending as well as unflattering answers to simple questions of information. . . . He is certainly a beguiling figure. It is a question whether any other double-dealer ever went undetected half so long."[37]

Gulliver's limited vision results in "a stacking of cards" that inclines the argument toward the negative. Thus in book 4, as in book 2, when the host draws a line under the evidence that Swift has allowed Gulliver to reveal, his statement of what it all adds up to is inevitably and crashingly unflattering: ". . . he looked upon us as sort of animals to whose share, by what accident he could not conjecture, some small pittance of Reason had fallen, whereof we made no other use than by its assistance to aggravate our *natural* corruptions, and to acquire new ones which nature had not given us" (4:7). This time, Gulliver agrees with his host: "When I thought of my family, my friends, my countrymen, or [the] human race in general, I considered them as they really were, Yahoos in shape and disposition, perhaps a little more civilized, and qualified with the gift of speech, but making no other use of reason than to improve and multiply those vices whereof their brethren in this country had only the share that nature allotted them" (4:10).

It is as a thorough misanthrope that Gulliver returns home. When his loving wife greets him affectionately, he swoons, "having not been used to the touch of that odious animal [his wife!] for so many years." The swoon lasts a long time, "almost an hour," for Gulliver's revulsion is now compounded. His wife has a "smell" which is not only (as with the perfumed Brobdingnagian maidens) physically overpowering, but is now also (at least for him) morally unbearable. She is a Yahoo. He never even asks about their baby, born after he left home.

Gulliver's Travels ends with what is generally agreed to be a searing indictment of mankind. Gulliver himself states what has happened: ". . . the many virtues of those excellent quadrupeds [the Houyhnhnms] placed in opposite view to human corruptions, had so far opened my eyes and enlarged my understanding, that I began to view the actions and passions of man in a very different light, and to think the honour of my own kind not worth managing" (4:7). It is a dramatic high point in the narrative. Gulliver has come to regard his fellows in about the same way that Conrad regards his "papier-mâché Mephistopheles" in *Heart of Darkness:* "If I tried I could poke my forefinger through him, and would find nothing inside but a little loose dirt, maybe."

The Curtain of Gloom

I am convinced that Swift would not have entirely endorsed Gulliver's terrible indictment, though he surely had moments when he felt that it was true, and I have tried in this chapter to call attention to some of these moments. There are innumerable times and there are innumerable places when men and women do unquestionably behave like Yahoos, and Swift was perfectly well aware of this. He knew that people do not always behave this way, however, so the curtain of gloom has not fallen here, as I believe it did in the *Tale* volume and was to fall again, later in Swift's life. So, though Swift would have understood why Gulliver spoke so bitterly, it is impossible for me to believe that Swift would have applauded Gulliver's reaction to that final indictment. There are good reasons for making this assertion.

One major reason is that Swift shows us that Gulliver is wrong on several counts. All men in the world defined by this book are not Yahoos. Pedro de Mendez, the captain in whose ship Gulliver travels back to Europe, is by Gulliver's own description "a very courteous and generous person." Gulliver therefore "descended to treat him like an animal which had some little portion of reason." To say that Swift intended Don Pedro as a kind of test of Gulliver's judgment is obviously a thesis beyond demonstration. It suggests a more sophisticated narrative skill than most people would credit Swift with. However, Don Pedro does in fact serve as a test, whether Swift intended it or not; and it is a test that Gulliver fails. A writer could hardly more clearly indicate Gulliver's sorry status as a reporter. Readers will recall how seemingly trustworthy Gulliver was in the account of his first voyage, though even then there was need for caution. Gulliver was naive; he exaggerated; he "said the thing that was not." Yet he had not at that point entirely forfeited our trust in him as a reporter. The Gulliver who thinks Don Pedro de Mendez is "an animal" has. We therefore are right to question his belief that he has discovered the absolute truth, rather than a qualified truth, in the land of the Houyhnhnms; and we are certainly right to think that his reaction to his discovery is preposterous. Swift has to be laughing at this crazy chap who becomes so enamored of his friendly horses that "he fell to imitate their gait and gesture, which is now grown into a habit." What a fool Gulliver has become.

Also, in important ways Gulliver is really quite wrong about his

Houyhnhnms. Though possessing some ideal traits, his hosts are not wholly ideal and I cannot believe Swift intended them to be so. They are ideal in that "Friendship and Benevolence are [their] two principal virtues." And they "excell all other mortals in poetry," says Gulliver, suddenly a qualified judge in these matters. But such traits would hardly seem to make them the "perfection of nature" when we learn that they do not cry, they do not laugh, they do not love; they cannot read or write; and I believe that Swift had to be snorting with derision when he heard Gulliver, parting from his master, say, "I took . . . leave of my master; but as I was going to prostrate myself to kiss his hoof, he did me the honour to raise it gently to my mouth." A delightfully ridiculous picture! Gulliver continues (Swift, behind him, being ironical), "Detractors are pleased to think it improbable, that so illustrious a person should descend to give so great a mark of distinction to a creature so inferior as I"—"Illustrious a *person*"?!

Frank Brady remarks that "for all their qualities, the Houyhnhnms are odd at the edges, so to speak."[38] Many studies have helped to settle this point. Ernest Tuveson has suggested that Swift's religious convictions, convictions that he held strongly and sincerely, would obviously prevent him from offering the Houyhnhnms to us as ideal.[39] This may in part be so, but the suggestion would be more convincing if Swift had a different collection of religious convictions. As Louis Landa has pointed out, "It is hardly necessary to mention again that [Swift's] concern was less with spiritual or doctrinal affairs than with temporal."[40]

Moreover, in addition to those matters noted above, there is the fact that the whole idea of the Houyhnhnms, as metaphor, would have presented Swift with problems, had he intended them to be regarded as ideal, as Gulliver thought they were. A reader tends to identify himself with that which an author considers attractive, if he respects the author. But it is not likely that many adult readers, in their right mind, would hope that some day they could be like horses. Virtues may be convincingly personified; if any degree of sophistication is desired, they cannot be convincingly "horse-ified."

Thus a repetition of a point made above: at this time in his life Swift could not approve Gulliver's terrible indictment as an absolute truth, but he could give it a qualified endorsement since he himself often felt much as Gulliver did. But Swift could not approve Gulliver's insane reaction to that indictment. These assertions get some support, it has been suggested, by Swift's underlining his narrator's unreliability: Gulliver calls the demonstrably good Pedro de Mendez an animal, which he is not; he considers the horse the very model of perfection, which they are not; and he puts his readers in the untenable position of thinking that a horse can convincingly personify human virtues.

With all this evidence and all these opinions before us, what can we now conclude about this fantastic journey to the land of the Houyhn-hnms? Frank Brady assures us that "violent arguments about the mean-ing of part 4 seem inevitable."[41] Wayne Booth tells us that this fourth book is not "easily decipherable."[42] Nobody could argue with either judgment. Also, as indicated earlier in this chapter, James Clifford refers to a division between those who prefer a "hard" approach to their interpretation and those, like me, who prefer a "soft" approach. That is, I am one of those who find what Clifford calls "comic overtones" throughout *Gulliver's Travels,* and I do not regard the book's conclusion as unqualifiably tragic. Each responsible reader will try to come to his own conclusion, however, and from reader to reader, conclusions will vary because of the readers' various backgrounds in reading and experi-ence, their various temperaments, and their fondness for this or that critical approach. Finally, any conclusion that can be textually verified will command respect. I offer now the conclusion to which this chapter has been pointing for some time, and I offer it with the reminder that a number of other conclusions—wise and interesting; "soft" or "hard"— are available to the student who wants to pursue this question further.

The substance of this conclusion, already noted above, is simply that Swift has two satiric butts in book 4: man and Gulliver. Man always can be, and too often is, as Gulliver points out in book 4, "a lump of deformity and diseases, both in body and mind, smitten with pride." In other words, man can be a Yahoo and is, in fact, often worse than a Yahoo. On the evidence that Gulliver offers, he was right, and to the extent that Swift agreed with him, man is indeed a butt of his satire. What Swift seems also to be saying at the end of his book, however, is that Gulliver's reaction to his corrosive indictment is made by a re-porter whose judgment cannot be trusted. He cannot be trusted be-cause he is insane. When Gulliver swoons "for almost an hour" when his wife embraces him, his reaction is that of an insane person. Equally neurotic is the way he treats his family: five years after his return, they are still not allowed to touch his bread or drink out of the same cup, or even to take him by the hand. Gulliver all this while back home in England, "trots like a horse"; he spends four hours every day talking to his horses. He is obviously trying to force to reality this impossible metaphor (he = horse) in a frenetic attempt to avoid that other equally

wrong metaphor (he = Yahoo). His reaction to his complete disenchant-
ment with mankind is ludicrous. When last seen, therefore, he is an
object of amused contempt and the other butt of Swift's satire in this
book 4. As Professor Ross states, Gulliver at this point has "gone off
the deep end and cannot recover himself from the nightmare view of
man."[43]

By way of summary: the satire of book 4 of *Gulliver's Travels* is two
edged: it is against all men, whenever they are mean or self-polluted or
prideful; against Gulliver (or anyone like him) for an absurd response to
the discovery of what seems to him to be the true nature of man.

Chapter Seven

Recapitulation and Assessment

Something is known of what Swift looked like, and perhaps here is a good time to note the details. He was about five and a half feet tall—a bit below average by present-day standards—and in maturity given to plumpness and a double-chin. He had a sallow complexion, heavy eyebrows, and "eyes of wall,"[1] that is, prominent and bulging eyes. Contemporary reports inform us that his voice was strong and sharp, though not graceful or harmonious.[2]

We know quite a lot, too, about Swift's limitations. Apparently he knew little about and had no particular interest in music, painting, architecture, or dancing. He knew next to nothing about the cleansing effect of laughing at oneself. He could be stingy, sharp-tongued, demanding, overbearing, unctious, devious, and cruel. His life and writings abound with inconsistencies and paradoxes. As a sampling of these, consider only that he distrusted and was contemptuous of the mob's ability to decide anything rightly, but he could also assert that "God has given the bulk of mankind a capacity to understand reason when it is fairly offered."[3] He could in *Gulliver's Travels* (3:8) denounce "prostitute writers" who distort history, but he could himself distort the facts in *The Conduct of the Allies,* and he could tell Stella that his *New Journey to Paris* was "a formal grave lie, from beginning to end."[4] He could indignantly protest when Harley, Lord Oxford, gave him money, as though he were a paid hireling of the government, but his actions make it clear that he fully expected to be rewarded for his services. After he got his deanery, he told Stella that he would be hurt, financially, "unless the Queen will give me £1,000. I am sure she owes me a great deal more."[5]

In a memorable scene in her *Orlando,* Virginia Woolf reports an evening when Swift "walks in unannounced" and thunders out some lines from book 4 of *Gulliver's Travels.* Orlando interrupts: "But stop, stop your iron pelt of words, lest you flay us all alive, and yourself too!" Then follows this insightful authorial comment: "Nothing can be plainer than that violent man. He is so coarse and yet so clean; so brutal, yet so kind; scorns the whole world, yet talks baby language to a girl, and will die, can we doubt it, in a madhouse."[6] Wrong about the place of Swift's death, Woolf was right about everything else. The man's paradoxes and inconsistencies were what she was referring to.

Yet despite all these curious and sometimes unsettling details that we know about, it is on record that Swift was loved and respected by a large group of good and loyal friends, many of whom were numbered among the most distinguished people of his England and Ireland. Among these friends he was thought to be a valuable and cheerful companion who loved to call out, "*Vive la bagatelle!*" (Let nonsense reign!); George Berkeley called him "one of the best natured and agreeable men in the world."[7] Finally, we know that he was idolized by the Irish people.

Despite all the knowledge that the biographers have given us, however, I suspect that Swift, the man and his works, will remain forever something of a puzzle. Any fairly representative collection of books about him reveal how earnestly and persistently has been the search for an answer to these puzzles. The search has concentrated on finding a pattern in the life and writings and trying to calculate what this pattern means. Thus we have books like *Swift, or the Egotist,* where part of the title (*the Egotist*) suggests an answer to the major puzzles, as do other such titular epithets: *The Conjured Spirit, Giant in Chains, Preacher and Jester, The Brave Desponder, Romantic and Cynic Moralist, A Hypocrite Reversed.* However excellent such studies are, I see danger in applying any all-embracing epithet to the life and writings of so complex a figure as Swift. There is always something, and sometimes quite a lot, left out or left over.

Surely to a degree Swift did, or was, or exemplified all of what the titles suggest; but, when these and books under scores of other titles have been read, many questions somehow manage to be with us still. Some of these questions are homely little ones that we do not have to worry too much about, though the answers might surprise us. Did Swift ever kiss a baby or hold one in his arms? Did Swift ever cry? Did he ever notice a sunset? Did he ever sit with a purring cat in his lap (like Samuel Johnson with a cat he had named Hodge)? Swift had a couple of dogs that apparently he brought along on visits. (On one occasion during one of his visits, his hostess, Lady Acheson, referred to his "Brace of Puppies how they stuff, / And they must have three Meals a Day").[8] What were the dogs' names? What breed(s)? Nobody knows.

Doubtless other and more important questions there are, and among them is the perennial puzzle of Swift's relationship with women, particularly with Varina Waring, Esther Johnson, and Esther Vanhomrigh. We wonder why, when he was young and living with Sir William Temple, he did not more vigorously prosecute the advancement of his own career. Why did he "renounce" poetry in 1693? Why did not the chief ministers of the kingdom—his close friends, he thought—push harder for his advancement? What was the reason for delaying the publication of the *Tale* volume? How accurately does the imagery of the *Tale* volume, and elsewhere, reveal his deep-seated, unarticulated, but nonetheless very real convictions about humankind? Did he or did he not marry Esther Johnson (Stella)? Of the many sermons that he preached, why are we left with so few? Even if he was careless with his sermon manuscripts and deemed them of no great consequence, there were plenty of people around who could be presumed to treasure them and want to profit from them. Swift was very careless with his poetry manuscripts, but three volumes of poetry in Sir Harold Williams's edition testify to the interest that other people had in collecting and putting into print any and every scrap of Swift's verse that they could get hold of. Why did they not do the same with his sermons? Why do we have only eleven or twelve of them? Again, what interpretation should we give to the "little language" in *The Journal To Stella* and in *Gulliver's Travels?* Larger questions, relevant to any great literary work, also still abide: specifically what is the meaning of *Gulliver's Travels,* or of *A Tale of a Tub,* or of *The Modest Proposal,* or of *The Journal to Stella,* or of "Verses on the Death of Dr. Swift," and so on, through all the list of great productions. I have attempted in this book to comment on many of these questions and to answer them as best I could. Other biographers and critics will find different, and I am entirely willing to believe, better answers, and other questions to answer; for many puzzles will always stubbornly remain, always to command our interest.

However, the known facts of Swift's life and the many goodly towers that are his literary productions do reveal a skyline, so to speak, that almost any reader of Swift would immediately recognize as "Swiftean." If part of this man and his work still resists our most persistent and studious inquiry, we can yet admit the existence of what Quintana called "a picture . . . reasonably complete and consistent."[9] Swift's major works of prose and poetry give this "reasonably complete" picture.

The *Tale* Volume

Each of the first major prose works may be read singly. However, similarities in tone, point of view, and major themes make it in some ways preferable to regard these three works—*A Tale of a Tub, The Battle of the Books,* and *The Mechanical Operation of the Spirit* (published in 1704 and 1710)—as contributing to one whole. So viewed, the *Tale* volume's dominant target is irrationality. Because man allows his "fancy" to get "astride his reason" and his "imagination" to be "at cuffs with his senses," "common understanding, as well as common sense, is kicked out of doors." Since it is clear that abuses in religion and in learning are inexorably the consequence of such irrational behavior, it must be granted that Swift succeeded with the intention he stated in the "Apology" to his 1710 edition of the *Tale:* "The abuses in Religion, he proposed to set forth in the Allegory of the Coats, and the three Brothers, which was to make up the body of the discourse. Those in learning he chose to introduce by way of digressions."

The *Tale* volume does achieve its announced intention, and it does have passages of absolutely scintillating brilliance, but it is not so widely read as in the book Swift wrote much later in life, *Gulliver's Travels* (published 1726). He wanted to vex readers of his *Travels,* and he did so, particularly in book 2 (where some readers were bored) and book 4 (where some were angered). But books 1 and 2 caused more delight than vexation and by and large still do. The sheer fun in *Gulliver's Travels* will, I think, always attract more readers than will the *Tale* volume. Also, the narrative and thematic tension of the *Travels* is more expertly sustained, and Gulliver, as narrator, is thought to be a more likable, a more convincing, and, to the general reader, a more recognizable figure than is the so-called modern hack who purports to be the writer of the *Tale* volume.

I suggest that the chief difficulty readers have with the *Tale* volume is the confusion caused by Swift's uncertain control of his materials. His book says more than he apparently intended it to say, and unfortunately this "more" sometimes contradicts the stated intentions of its author. Thus if he is to support the ancients in a "battle" against the moderns, he should not begin his account by insisting upon the triviality and animality of the whole affair. It is a crippling tactical blunder to assert on his opening page that "war is the child of pride," for the comment, if it is true at all, must obviously apply to this particular "battle"; furthermore, it is irreparably damaging to proclaim that, "to speak in the phrase of writers upon politics, we may observe in the Republic of Dogs (which, in its original seems to be an institution of the many) . . . that civil broils arise among them when it happens for one great bone to be seized on by some leading dog. . . ." The image does not even sort out the good "ancient" dogs from the bad "modern" dogs: the whole lot of them in this quarrel are just plain dogs. Again, though we must allow the fact that the *Tale* does sharply illuminate the nature of the abuses in religion and in learning, we must also allow that the satire strikes as hard at Swift's own church as it does at the churches he was presumably attacking; and, although we are willing to agree that the use of common sense would redress all abuses in religion and in learning, this hopeful possibility is precluded of attainment when in sections 8 and 9 of the *Tale* we learn that among us all we cannot muster so much as a thimbleful of common sense.

Perhaps if Swift had managed to keep enough distance between himself and his narrator he might have succeeded. But too often he allowed himself to be ensnared by his own intense involvement in the situation he was describing. The distance between him and his speaker (his tale teller) is as a consequence so slight and so very narrow that we are inclined to hear not the tale teller but Swift himself inform us (section 9) that "if we take an examination of what is generally understood by happiness, as it has respect either to the understanding or the senses, we shall find all its properties and adjuncts will herd under this short definition, that it is a perpetual possession of being well deceived." Though irony may well have been intended by the remark, it is an irony that, at least for some of us, does not succeed. Again (section 8) we hear not "the learned Aeolist maintain . . ." but Swift himself maintain that "the original cause of all things [is] wind, from which principle this whole universe was at first produced. . . ."

In a world so formed, there is no reason. Elsewhere in this text I have suggested the possibility that the nihilistic implications of the *Tale* volume are in part a reflection of its author's mood during the time of the book's composition. If he then thought that in his world there was no reason, it followed of course that there was no common sense available to sally out and be "at cuffs" with "fancy." Thus inextricably threaded into and through the fabric of the *Tale* volume are images and ideas that, refusing to be confined to Swift's too narrow statement of intention, end up in truth by revealing the inadequacies of that intention. The confusion is unsettling to many readers, and is perhaps the best reason that, while awed by its great high points, they feel at the last a dissatisfaction with this masterpiece.

The Poetry

A comparable dissatisfaction with Swift's poetry occurs if we are expecting too much or are looking for qualities that his poetry simply does not possess. There is no rapture and no lyric note; there is little use made of metaphor; and much of the poetry is quite trivially occasional—like an invitation to Dr. Sheridan to come to dinner, or like any other of the scores of inconsequential poems that he himself called "family trifles." However, even in some of the poems that have little or no poetic merit there are lines that are interesting as expression of themes dominant in the prose and in his thinking generally. "To Mr. Congreve" (1693), for example, compares critics to asses ("Nor need the lion's skin conceal the ass"), and this so familiar use of "*le mythe animal*" will appear in almost the same form in the "Digression concerning Critics" in *A Tale of a Tub* (1704). Also, in this same poem, Swift cuts at the pseudoscientism of "virtuosoes . . . dissecting flies," and this he does again more than thirty years later in book 3 of *Gulliver's Travels* (1726). Moreover, in the poetry he uses satiric methods that he also employs with superb effect in the prose works. One of his better poems, "A Beautiful Young Nymph" (1731), achieves much of its power because, just as in *Gulliver's Travels,* its author distorts reality by describing it only partially and then by exaggerating the features even of those parts. The distortion results in caricature, but it is not caricature that we can laugh at or be comfortable with. Its maker's fierce indignation and passionate conviction are too apt to compel a disturbing measure of agreement with his comment, "Who sees, will spew."

In recent years a remarkable increase in the scholarly and critical attention given to the poems seems, happily, to signal a wider interest in them. More readers are discovering that Swift's poetry deserves and rewards study. They are learning that, at its best, it can be wonderfully conversational and witty (as in "Verses on the Death of Dr. Swift") [1732]); it can be brilliantly and brutally satirical (as in the "Satirical Elegy on the Death of a Late Famous General" [1722] or "The Day of Judgement" [date unknown]; it can be teasing and tender (as in "Stella's Birth-day [1721]; and (as in the hilarious and earthy "Strephon and Chloe" [1731] or in "A City Shower" [1710] it can bring to a poem facts that the mainstream of poetry has tended to ignore. Almost everybody sees the rainbow after a city shower, if there is a rainbow; it is a rare man who, like Swift, pretty much ignores the rainbow and studies what is always there—the gutter—and notes, after the shower, "Sweepings from Butchers Stalls, Dung, Guts, and Blood, / Drown'd Puppies, Stinking Sprats, all drench'd in Mud, / Dead Cats and Turnip-Tops . . . tumbling down the Flood." These too are facts. Just look, and you will see. You will see the chamber pot beside the wedding bed, too.

Gulliver's Travels

About as much as anything ever can, *Gulliver's Travels* contributes to the "reasonably complete and consistent" picture of the enigmatic genius who envisaged the world that this book defines.

Book 1 of the *Travels* shows us an archetypal average man named Lemuel Gulliver who, in relation to the various forms of pettiness and meanness in Lilliput, seems commendably humane and good-hearted. Book 1 also introduces several problems that must be coped with early in a reading of that book. One of these, the problem of scatology (Swift's "excremental vision") has in the past infected and warped responses to the *Travels,* to the poems, and to much of the *Tale* volume. It need not do so today, though no doubt in some places it still does. Another problem has to do with Swift's topical satire, for—especially in books 1 and 3—he makes numerous and very specific references to men and events of his day. A knowledge of the considerable data that have immediate contemporary application does certainly add to our understanding of the book, but an awareness of such data is of secondary importance to an awareness of the satire that is timeless. Flimnap is to be sure Prime Minister Robert Walpole, but more importantly he is any politician who wins and maintains power solely by his adroitness in walking, or even doing tricks, on the political "tightrope." A third, oft-mentioned problem of the *Travels* is that of the "little language," which, though it attracts scholarly concern, must in the present state of knowledge be thought primarily, if not exclusively, merely an effective verisimilar device: this is how residents do talk in these make-believe lands. A final problem has to do with Swift's narrator, Gulliver, whose effectiveness as a narrator is so great that his only competition in the Swift canon is from the projector in *The Modest Proposal* or from "M.B.," the humble drapier. Gulliver is a likable, fairly responsible reporter whom we want to trust completely but never quite can and whom, at the end of the fourth voyage, we have to regard as incompetent.

Book 1 introduces major satiric themes, too, like the satire on the ingratitude of princes and on the empty pomposity of titles. The Lilliputian emperor, whose height is all of six and a half inches, has eight names to carry around: Golbasto Momaren Evlame Gurdilo Shefin Mully Ully Gue. The burden, especially of those last three names, is enough to crush an ordinary man; but this nobleman, who is "taller," Gulliver absurdly reports, "than the sons of men," seems pleased with the premise that the bigger the title, the bigger the man. Obviously this small chap and his subjects needed Montaigne's healthy reminder, in "Of Experience": "So it is no use for us to mount on stilts, for on stilts we must still walk with our own legs. And in the loftiest throne in the world we are still sitting on our own behind."

Book 1 has other satiric targets. There are the travelers who, as hosts, torture guests with tiresome and almost endless recitals of everything about their trip, including their bowel movements. There are the trivial arguments in religion and in politics about which Swift seems to be saying, "When we argue these matters, let us not make a religious issue over which end of an egg should be broken first; or a political argument over what kind of heels to wear on our shoes: argument in these areas should be over matters of more import." Finally, chapter 6 of book 1 raises to prominence a central question that poor Gulliver will not even recognize as a question for years and a question that, once recognized, he will not attempt to answer until late in his last voyage. The question is, Will this world-traveler, seeing near-utopian civilization in this chapter, notice any difference between this vision and the civilization of his own world? Will he compare? Will he assess? At the end of book 1, Gulliver makes no assessment. The voyage has taught him nothing, so far as we can tell.

Book 2 continues with familiar Swiftean themes. The need for personal cleanliness is once more expressed (in chapters 1 and 4) and echoes his advice to the young friend in *The Letter to a Young Lady* (1723): wash often enough and thoroughly enough to avoid the charge of being at once "very fine and very filthy." Most important in this book, however, is the contrast between Gulliver's moral stature and the moral stature of his hosts. That they tower both physically and *morally* over Gulliver is most vividly seen in a confrontation scene when, on the basis of evidence Gulliver has furnished him, the large-souled Brobdingnagian ruler dispassionately concludes that "the bulk of your natives [are] the most pernicious race of little odious vermin that nature ever suffered to crawl upon the face of the earth." The indictment astonishes Gulliver, who can only attribute its severity to "a certain *narrowness of thinking,* from which we and the politer countries of Europe are wholly exempted." (Note in passing how perfectly successful Swift's irony can be and very often is!) Gullible Gulliver is still the *ingenu* in this cast of characters. This voyage, like the first one, has taught him nothing.

The Gulliverian mask is used in book 3 so very incidentally that it might as well be ignored; for the most part Swift in this book speaks in his own person. Satiric themes are, again, themes that a reader has come to recognize as part of the pattern of Swift's thought: the refusal to accept as scientific all activity that is called scientific; the satire on false and useless learning; the abuse of human talents employed to trivial ends; and the opposition to English tyranny—an opposition that Swift had expressed less allegorically but even more forcefully in 1724, with the fourth of *The Drapier Letters,* wherein he had written, "By the laws of God, of NATURE, of NATIONS, and of your own Country, you ARE and OUGHT to be as FREE a People as your Brethren in England."

In addition, as noted earlier, book 3 ridicules "prostitute" historians who pretend to be "truly informed of the springs and motives of great enterprises"; and in a notable section it satirizes naive ideas about immortality. Finally, implicit in book 3, just as in so much of his other major writings, is the insistence on the paramount importance of the mind and on the imperative need to see beneath the surface of things. Such Swiftean touchstones appear also in "Stella's Birth-day" (1721), and in *The Letter to a Young Gentleman* (1720), and often in the *Tale* volume (1704 and 1710); but such reminders are misleading if they suggest that the themes are anything less than persuasive in the Swift lexicon.

Book 4 of *Gulliver's Travels* finds Gulliver confronting two sharply defined distortions. The first of these distortions is the description of the Houyhnhnm masters: to Gulliver they appear to be perfection, and he accepts this appearance as the truth of the matter. The other distortion insists that Gulliver in all essentials looks like, and in fact is, a Yahoo. This is an image Gulliver at first strenuously resists. The resistance ends and the climax comes when a female Yahoo, "inflamed by desire," attempts to violate Gulliver when he has stripped himself naked in order to bathe. The attempt precipitates the humbling admission that relieves the major tension of the entire four books: "now I could no longer deny that I was a real Yahoo in every line and feature, since the females had a natural propensity to me, as one of their own species." If Gulliver is Yahoo—if Everyman is Yahoo—then the civilization that he and Everyman represent is also Yahoo. In the dim light of the Houyhnhnm culture, and with help of "lectures" from his Houyhnhnm master and the "discources of him and his friends," Gulliver thus finally assesses the worth of his own civilization in terms of what he believes his travels have taught him: "When I thought of my family, my friends, my countrymen, or human race in general, I considered them as they really were, Yahoos in shape and disposition, perhaps a little more cultivated and qualified with the gift of speech, but making no more use of reason than to improve and multiply those vices whereof their brethren [the Yahoos] in this country [the land of the Houyhnhnms] had only the share that nature allotted them."

As I have argued in the previous chapter, Swift certainly thought he had reason often enough to sympathize with, and even to a degree to endorse, Gulliver's conclusion. But I do not think he entirely did so. In the mid-1720s he was, I believe, about as content with his lot as ever he could be. Stella was not well; Ireland was in a depression; but Esther Vonhomrigh's death had ended her long unhappiness, and some of Swift's, too; the dean was happy with his circle of friends; things were going well at his cathedral; and *Gulliver's Travels* was in the making. I therefore do not see him giving way to Gulliver's final bitter and despairing assessment of the human condition. Still and all he does not ridicule Gulliver for thinking as he does; rather, he ridicules him for his absurd and outrageous reaction to this way of thinking; in short, to his reaction to the discovery of what he considers to be the true nature of his fellows.

Full freighted with neuroses, an unhappy and misanthropic Gulliver left the land of the horses on 15 February 1714–15, at nine o'clock in the morning. The sorrel nag ("who always loved me," he reports) whinnied (Gulliver says "cried"!) after him, "Hnuy illa nyha majah Yahoo." Once home, Gulliver trots like a horse and spends four hours a day talking with the two horses he keeps in his stable. The Gulliver who has concluded that he and all his fellows are Yahoos is obviously unhinged; therefore I cannot suppose that Swift wants us to believe that Gulliver's final corrosive indictment was unqualifiedly his (Swift's) view—or should be ours.

Assessment

Students often protest that Swift's writings lose a dimension by one striking omission: they do not explicitly give any positive and affirmative solutions to the problems that the author posed with such startling clarity. Thus in *Gulliver's Travels* Swift shows us what our response should *not* be, but he does not show us what our response *should* be, if a clear-sighted view of the human condition perforce drives us also to a conclusion as bleak as his. Consequently, this book and his other principal writings seem to some critics to achieve their greatest brilliance by a solely negative impact. F. R. Leavis says, "We have, then, in [Swift's] writings probably the most remarkable expression of negative feelings and attitudes that literature can offer—the spectacle of creative powers . . . exhibited consistently in negation and in rejection."[10]

The negations do imply affirmations, however, and these affirmations are not hard to find in *Gulliver's Travels* or, indeed, in anything Swift ever wrote. The affirmations are the sort that we might expect from a man whose custom it was to celebrate his birthday by reading Job 3:3: "Let the day perish wherein I was born, and the night in which it was said, 'There is a man child conceived.' " The affirmative aspect of *Gulliver's Travels* will never incite anybody to write lyric poems about bird-watching or motherhood, but the affirmations are nonetheless there. In truth it is not difficult to see at least something of them in all of Swift's major prose and poetry—and fairly satisfactorily to explain their meaning and impact. No doubt this meaning and this impact are not exactly the same for all readers, for each reader must inevitably respond somewhat differently to any literary work.

Inevitably and necessarily, however, a person rising from a reading of a great writer and his works will try to find a fairly specific place in what seems to him a sane area of interpretation; he tries to make some sort of final evaluation of what the writings of this great figure amount to, today—though even as he makes the judgment, he is aware of how hazardous and inadequate such attempts always are. In attempting to reach a sensible assessment of those writings of Swift that are most read in our times—and an assessment consistent with the positions taken in earlier pages of this book—I begin by trying to understand something about Swift's distorted vision. Probably that is the place to begin with any artist, for distortion, at least in the sense of limitation of focus, is essential to art. Also, distortion is a relative matter that defines the uniqueness of each of us: it is the way each of us has of looking at things.

Swift's way of seeing things—his distortion—is marked in the main by two attributes. The first might be called the "dead cat" syndrome, for after a heavy rain storm he saw "Dead Cats" drowned in the gutter. He also saw there the "Dung, Guts, and Blood," and the "Drown'd Puppies, Stinking Sprats, all drench'd in Mud." Those are the types of things Swift noticed, I am quite sure he would never in his life have seen William Carlos Williams's homely-lovely "red wheel / barrow / glazed with rain / water / beside the white chickens." Looking at a Brobdingnagian female nursing a baby, Swift's little Gulliver saw what, and only what he himself would have seen: the "monstrous breast" with a "nipple . . . about half the bigness of my head . . . and the dug so varified with spots, pimples and freckles, that nothing could appear more nauseous." This is the only detail he gives us about the appearance of this woman; and, though it is a distortion that is a caricature, it is also an honest bit of reporting. Confronted by this huge and horrid dug, who could honestly pretend not to be looking at it? Occasionally, in other words, Swift's distorted vision (his genius) saw exactly the single repulsive detail that so dominates a picture that it destroys any chance of, in fact almost eliminates any reason for, a fairer, fuller, and a more tolerant view.

Another attribute of Swift's vision might be termed his "peeled orange" syndrome. He seemed driven to peel away the outside of things, for the outside is a fraud that cheats us of the truth. So we must stand by to see a woman "flayed" and, in our innocence, be surprised "how much it altered her person for the worse" (section 9 of *The Tale*). If we see "the carcass of a beau" stripped, we will be "all amazed to find so many unsuspected faults under one suit of clothes." Swift will insist that we make a prostitute remove not only her finery, but everything; for only then will we discover her "shancres [cankers], issues, [and] running sores" ("A Beautiful Young Nymph Going to Bed"). We must hound out of business a charlatan named John Partridge, whose almanacs attacked the clergy of the Church of England; but we must realize that the real reason this charlatan is more than merely a silly joke is that he pretends in his prophecies to a knowledge he does not have. So we must be made not only to see him as he is—a hypocrite—but to care about truthful seeing.

These two attributes of Swift's vision enabled him in his best works to seize unerringly upon the single most telling detail, or pattern of details, in any situation. Sometimes it is only in retrospect that we recognize his technique and realize the nature of his distortions. Readers of his works, however, usually find that protest is forestalled by Swift's sure conviction that, as part of his community of reasonable men and women, his readers care about the things that he cares about: therefore he will assume that they understand and approve his dry ironies and sardonic asides; that they also share unreservedly and completely in his concern, his anxiety, his distress, his revulsion, or his hatred. In his greatest writings, it is the distress, the revulsion, and the hatred that are most insistently communicated; for he was a man who relived with a frequently quite terrible intensity each moment that, recollecting, he chose to record. The totality of moments is salted with fun and frolic, to be sure; but the final impression is not so much negative as merely grim, since the threshold of hope in a world where "happiness . . . is a perpetual possession of being well-deceived" (section 9 of *The Tale*) is predictably low. It is so low that Swift's addiction to the thesis that reason is the cure-all is properly regarded as a theme sincerely expressed but with its subtleties largely unexamined; in short, to a degree illusionary. Far more convincing are his pronouncements about the baleful effects of folly, or absence of reason, and the overriding need to get beneath the surface of things, for only then—this positive exhortation avers—will we see things as they really are.

But also at the heart of Swift's teaching is the affirmation that I think is his most valuable contribution to our times: it is the affirmation that a clear and honest view of life will show how rare and how spectacular is the triumph that manages to hold its own against the forces of dirt, of pretense, of pride, and of evil in our world. Man's odds against these forces being so nearly hopeless, his most stunningly victorious accomplishments must necessarily be simple ones: as the Brobdingnagian king in *Gulliver's Travels* puts it, to make "two blades of grass to grow upon a spot of ground where only one grew before" (book 2:6).

For some readers the affirmation implicit in the Brobdingnagian king's remark is not relieved by a reading of Swift's other most important literary productions. It is not, I confess, for me. At least at the same time, however, its pessimism is significantly commented on by outside biographical data. Gulliver's response to his vision was neurotic. Swift's response to his vision was to spend many of his best moments, for the best part of a half century, as a priest of the Church of Ireland.

However, even as note is taken of the vocation to which he for so many years gave himself, I recall his comment to Charles Ford (22 June

1736): "I have long given up all hopes of Church or Christianity."[11] It is true that Swift's latest years were filled with sadness as the curtain of gloom gradually closed in on his world, yet until at least the early 1730s he had not yet relinquished the obstinate hope, I feel, that he might yet get the other blade of grass to grow. Later in the same year of the depressing letter to Charles Ford he sent this note to his doctor, John Nichols:

Sir,
    You attended a monstrous haunch of venison to the deanery; and if you and Mrs. Nicholls do not attend it again to-morrow, it shall be thrown into the streets; therefore all excuses must be laid aside. Mrs. Whiteway and I shall be all your company, and I will give you a pot of ale to relish it.
    I am, with true esteem, Sir, your most obedient humble servant, J. Swift.[12]

This sort of letter is not written by a man who has given up all hope.
    Whatever Swift may have thought of his contemporaries in Ireland, crowds of them continued to celebrate his birthday and continued to believe that he lived his life "for the universal improvement of mankind." In such terms, at any rate, I find the best possible explanation of the obituary that his printer George Faulkner wrote in the *Dublin Journal,* just after his friend's death. It bespeaks great admiration and affection:

Last Saturday [19 October 1745] at three o'clock in the Afternoon dyed that great and eminent Patriot the Rev. Dr. Jonathan Swift, Dean of St. Patrick's Dublin, in the 78th Year of his Age. . . . His Genius, Works, Learning, and Charity are so universally admired, That for a News Writer to attempt his Character would be the highest Presumption. Yet as the Printer hereof is proud to acknowledge his infinite Obligations to that Prodigy of Wit, he can only lament, that he is by no Means equal to so bold an undertaking.

Without diminishing Swift, the modest Faulkner's warm obituary does perhaps simplify him more than the record really permits. To keep the record accurate, I will allow that, though the outlines of Faulkner's pattern are clear and consistent enough, my understanding of the nature of this man and of the techniques and quality of his writings are instinct still with unsolved puzzles. It is inevitably so, I suspect, for truly, as Esther Vanhomrigh said in one of her letters to him, "never any one liveing thought like you."[13] Miss Vanhomrigh had learned the hard way that genius is fascinating but finally inexplicable.

Notes and References

Chapter One

1. Herbert Davis et al., eds., *The Prose Works of Jonathan Swift,* 16 vols. (Oxford: Basil Blackwell, 1939–74), 2:145.

2. Ibid., 155.

3. Ibid., 161.

4. Ricardo Quintana, *The Mind and Art of Jonathan Swift* (London: Oxford University Press, 1936), 364.

5. Elbert Hubbard, *Little Journeys to the Homes of the Great* (New York: G. P. Putman's Sons, 1895), 142–43.

6. Phyllis Greenacre, *Swift and Carroll, a Psychoanalytic Study of Two Lives* (New York: International Universities Press, 1955), 92.

7. Ibid., 101.

8. Irvin Ehrenpreis, *Swift: The Man, His Works, and The Age,* 3 vols. (London: Methuen & Co., 1962 [vol. 1]; 1967 [vol. 2]; Cambridge: Harvard University Press, 1983 [vol. 3], 1:69.

9. Ibid., 62.

10. Ibid.

11. Davis, *Works,* 5:192.

12. David Nokes, *Jonathan Swift, a Hypocrite Reversed: A Critical Biography* (Oxford: Oxford University Press, 1985), 30.

13. Swift to Miss Jane Waring, in Harold Williams, ed., *The Correspondence of Jonathan Swift,* 5 vols. (Oxford: Clarendon Press, 1965), 1:21.

14. Nokes (*Jonathan Swift,* 38) comments on this letter: "[It] reads like a patient scold that a petulent uncle might send to a wayward nephew or neice."

15. Swift to Miss Jane Waring, Wiliams, *Correspondence,* 1:35–36.

16. Harold Williams, ed., *The Journal to Stella,* 2 vols. (Oxford: Clarendon Press, 1948), 1:xxix.

17. Davis, *Works,* 5:193.

18. Irvin Ehrenpreis, *The Personality of Swift* (London: Methuen & Co., 1958), 119.

19. Louis Landa, *Swift and the Church of Ireland* (Oxford: Clarendon Press, 1954), 53.

20. Davis, *Works,* 7:xxxiii.

21. Ehrenpreis, *Swift,* 2:728.

22. Ibid., 727.

23. Cited by Quintana, *Mind and Art,* 206.

24. "During the eighteenth century clerical preferment was a thing of the market-place" (Landa, *Swift and the Church of Ireland*, 193).

25. Swift to Bolingbroke, 21 March 1730, Williams, *Correspondence*, 3:383.

26. Williams, *Journal*, 2:262.

27. Ehrenpreis, *Swift*, 2:211.

28. "I seldom walk less than four miles, sometimes six, eight, ten or more . . . or, if it rains, I walk as much through the house, up and down stairs . . ." (Swift to John Barber, Williams, *Correspondence*, 5:118).

29. Ibid., 2:127.

30. Ibid., 2:330.

31. Davis, *Works*, 5:79. Davis does not date this piece. Presumably it was written before 1714, however, when Swift left England.

32. Cited in John Traugott's *Discussions of Jonathan Swift* (Boston: D. C. Heath & Co., 1962), 83, from George Orwell's *Shooting an Elephant and Other Essays*.

33. Ricardo Quintana, *Swift, an Introduction* (London: Oxford University Press, 1955), 124.

34. Cited by Quintana, *An Introduction*, 3.

35. Ehrenpreis, *The Personality of Swift*, 125.

36. Landa, *Swift and the Church of Ireland*, 192–93.

37. John Hawkesworth, *The Works of Jonathan Swift, D.D.*, 12 vols. (London: Printed for C. Bathurst and others, 1755), 1:45.

38. Swift to Alexander Pope, 9 February 1736, Williams, *Correspondence*, 5:4.

39. Thomas Sheridan, *The Life of the Rev. Dr. Jonathan Swift* (1784; rpt., New York: Garland Publishing Co., 1974), 429.

40. Ehrenpreis, *Swift*, 2:868.

41. Ehrenpreis, *The Personality of Swift*, 123.

42. Ibid., 129.

43. Hawkesworth, *Works*, 1:58.

44. Sir Walter Scott, *The Life of Swift*, from *The Miscellaneous Works*, 10 vols. (Edinburgh: Adam and Charles Black, 1861), 2:404.

45. Cited by Ehrenpreis, *Swift*, 3:919.

46. Herbert Read, *Collected Essays in Literary Criticism* (London: Faber & Faber, 1938), 196.

47. Ibid.

Chapter Two

1. R. M. Adams posits a collaborative authorship in his "Jonathan Swift, Thomas Swift, and the Authorship of *A Tale of a Tub*," *Modern Philology* 64 (1967):198–202.

2. A. C. Guthkelch and D. Nichol Smith, eds., *A Tale of a Tub* (Oxford: Clarendon Press, 1959), xiv.

3. Translated from Émile Pons, *Swift: les années de jeunesse et le "Conte du Tonneau"* (Strasbourg: Publications de la faculté des lettres de Strasbourg, 1925), 256. Here and throughout this study, the translations are my own.

4. Ehrenpreis, *Swift*, 1:62.

5. Guthkelch and Smith, 206, fn. 1.

6. See Ehrenpreis, *Swift*, 1:186, for a discussion of this matter. Also see Pons, *Swift* section 11, chapter 1.

7. See Guthkelch and Smith, xlviii, for speculation on this question.

8. Quintana, *Mind and Art*, 86–98.

9. Guthkelch and Smith, liv.

10. Pons, *Swift*, 245.

11. Ronald Paulson, *Theme and Structure in Swift's "Tale of a Tub"* (New Haven: Yale University Press, 1960), passim.

12. J. A. Downie, *Jonathan Swift: Political Writer* (London: Routledge & Kegan Paul, 1984), 95. My italics.

13. John Traugott, "A Tale of a Tub," in *The Character of Swift's Satire*, ed. Claude Rawson (Newark: University of Delaware Press, 1983), 84. Italics are Traugott's.

14. Pons, *Swift*, 332.

15. Ibid., 284.

16. Traugott, "A Tale," 88–89.

17. Ibid., 115.

18. Scott, *Miscellaneous Works*, 2:78.

19. Pons, *Swift*, 339.

20. Davis, *Works*, 1:xxx: "Swift suggested to his printer Benjamin Tooke that a Key should be . . . made up of quotations from Wotton's *Observations.*" Tooke did so.

21. Pons, *Swift*, 284.

22. Ibid., 281.

23. Of course the St. James's Library was chosen deliberately, for Richard Bentley was librarykeeper there.

24. Pons, referring to Temple's skill as a beekeeper, says that it "was perhaps the greatest skill he had" (*Swift*, 270).

25. For example, "Swift paid a lifetime allowance to a needy sister; he supported and regularly visited a widowed and distant mother" (Ehrenpreis, *Swift*, 1:3). His benevolences were in fact extensive.

26. J. A. Downie calls *The Battle of the Books* "the greatest prose mock-heroic in English" (*Jonathan Swift*, 105).

27. Ehrenpreis, *Swift*, 1:188. But see Pons's comment, too. Pons believed that in section 4 of the *Tale*, Peter became "a person with flesh and blood" (*Swift*, 376).

28. Traugott, "A Tale," 100.

29. C. M. Webster, "Swift's *Tale of a Tub* Compared with Earlier Satires of the Puritans," *PMLA* 47 (1932):171–78; see also, *PMLA* 48 (1933):1141–53.

30. Pons, *Swift,* 389.

31. Martin Price, *Swift's Rhetorical Art* (New Haven: Yale University Press, 1953), 91.

32. Traugott, "A Tale," 96–97.

33. Paulson, *Theme and Structure,* 91.

34. Ehrenpreis, *Swift,* 1:189. Ehrenpreis thought that "the good man" was probably Temple; some critics might question this. See, for example, A. C. Elias, *Swift at Moor Park* (Philadelphia: University of Pennsylvania Press, 1982), wherein traditional assumptions about the Swift–Temple relationship are questioned.

35. "The History of Martin," which is often inserted at the end of the *Tale* volume, is not Swift's.

36. Donald Bruce, *Radical Doctor Smollett* (London: Golancz, 1964), 234.

37. Cited by, among others, Landa, *Swift and the Church of Ireland,* xiv. Also note that at this time St. Patrick's had no steeple to look down upon, thus suggesting that the truth of the legend is in doubt.

38. Traugott, "A Tale," 100.

39. Pons, *Swift,* 384–85.

Chapter Three

1. Ehrenpreis, *Swift,* 2:420.

2. Davis, *Works,* 6:ix.

3. Cited by Ehrenpreis, *Swift,* 2:500.

4. Richard Bentley, *A Dissertation upon the Epistles of Phalaris* (London: 1817), 283–84.

5. Davis, *Works,* 4:xvi.

6. Williams, *Journal,* 1:7 and footnote.

7. Ibid., xliv and pages following, for a discussion of this point.

8. All *Journal* quotations are from the invaluable Williams edition.

9. The *Journal's* first editors inserted the word *Stella* here. There is no evidence to show that Swift had begun to call Esther Johnson by this name at this time. (See Williams, *Journal,* 1:xxiv.)

10. Ehrenpreis, *Swift,* 2:641–47.

11. William Henry Irving, *The Providence of Wit in the English Letter Writers* (Durham: Duke University Press, 1955), 202–3.

12. Ehrenpreis, *Swift,* 2:661.

13. Williams, *Journal,* 1:xxxvi.

14. Ehrenpreis, *Swift,* 1:49.

15. See, for example, Denis Johnston, *In Search of Swift* (Dublin: Hodges Figgis & Co., 1959).

16. Nokes, *Jonathan Swift,* 218, fn.

Chapter Four

1. Harold Williams, *The Poems of Jonathan Swift,* 3 vols. (Oxford: Clarendon Press, 1958), 1:xvii. All quotations from Swift's poems are taken from one or another of the three volumes of this superb edition.

2. The books are by Nora Jaffe (1977), John Fischer (1978), Peter Schakel (1978), A. B. England (1980), and Louise Barnett (1981). See my Selected Bibliography.

3. Ehrenpreis, *Swift,* 1:120–30; Pons, *Swift,* 177; Williams, *Poems,* 1:xv.

4. Quintana, *Mind and Art,* 29. Herbert Davis refers to these early poems as "not . . . as weak or uninteresting as is often suggested" in *Jonathan Swift, Essays on His Satire* (New York: Oxford University Press, 1964), 172.

5. The four odes usually ascribed to Swift are "Ode to the Athenian Society," "Ode to the King on his Irish Expedition," "Ode to Sir William Temple," and "Ode to Dr. William Sancroft." All were written about 1692.

6. Swift to Thomas Swift, 3 May 1692, Williams, *Correspondence,* 1:8.

7. Ibid., 9.

8. Ibid., 10.

9. Cited by Henry Craik, *The Life of Jonathan Swift* (London: John Murray, 1832), 31.

10. Pons, *Swift,* 178.

11. For further details see Maurice Johnson, "A Literary Chestnut: Dryden's 'Cousin Swift,' " *PMLA* 67 (1952):1024–34.

12. Davis, *Swift, Essays on His Satire,* 171–72.

13. Quintana, *Introduction,* 49–50.

14. Joseph Horrell, *The Collected Poems of Jonathan Swift,* 2 vols. (London: Routledge & Kegan Paul, 1958), 1:xxx–xxxi.

15. Williams, *Journal,* 10 October 1710; other references are found under 12, 20 October; 2, 8, 10, 28, and 30 November; and 14 December 1710.

16. Ehrenpreis, *Swift,* 2:386. This critic also adds that in the "sharp observations of street life" the Irishman [Swift] was "showing off his familiarity with the English scene" (384). I do not believe it.

17. Roger Savage, "Swift's Fallen City: A Description of the Morning," in *Essential Articles for the Study of Jonathan Swift's Poetry,* ed. David Vieth (Hamden, Conn.: Archon Books, 1984), 143.

18. Patricia Spacks, *Eighteenth-Century Poetry* (Englewood Cliffs, N.J.: Prentice-Hall, 1964), xxxiii–xxxiv.

19. Brendon O Hehir, "Meaning of Swift's 'Description of a City Shower,' in Vieth, ed., *Essential Articles,* 118.

20. Quintana, *Mind and Art,* 278.

21. Cited by Scott, *Miscellaneous Works,* 2:272.

22. Quintana, *Mind and Art,* 221.

23. George Birbeck Hill, ed., *Johnson's Lives of the English Poets,* 3 vols. (Oxford: Clarendon Press, 1905), 3:31–32.

24. Quintana, *Introduction,* 19.

25. Hill, *Johnson's Lives,* 3:32.

26. Williams, *Poems,* 2:684.

27. Quintana, *Mind and Art,* 238.

28. Williams, *Correspondence,* 2:33–64.

29. Ibid., 3:130.

30. Horrell, *Collected Poems,* 1:xxxi.

31. Downie, *Jonathan Swift,* 173.

32. Cited by Horrell, *Collected Poems,* 1:lvi–lvii.

33. Ibid., lix.

34. Williams, *Poems,* 1:296.

35. Ibid., 2:577–78.

36. Landa, *Swift and the Church of Ireland,* 91.

37. 20 April 1731, Williams, *Correspondence,* 3: 458; 456.

38. Craik, *Life of Swift,* 499.

39. Williams, *Correspondence,* 3:501.

40. Nokes, *Jonathan Swift,* 365.

41. Norman Brown, "The Excremental Vision," in *Life against Death: The Psychoanalytical Meaning of History* (Middletown, Conn.: Wesleyan University Press, 1959), 179.

42. Ibid., 183. See also Nokes, *Jonathan Swift,* 372. Ehrenpreis also comments on the use "constantly reappearing in Swift's poems," of "imagery of filth" (*Swift,* 2:29).

43. See comments by Maurice Johnson, *The Sin of Wit* (Syracuse: Syracuse University Press, 1950), 110.

44. Ibid., 116.

45. John M. Aden, "Corinna and the Sterner Muse of Swift," in *Essential Articles,* ed. David Veith, 217.

46. Johnson, *Sin of Wit,* 35.

47. Williams, *Poems,* 1:xvi.

48. Ibid., *Correspondence,* 6:114–16.

49. Nokes, *Jonathan Swift,* 360.

50. Richard Rodino, "Blasphemy or Blessing? Swift's 'Scatological' Poems," in *Essential Articles,* ed. David Veith, 256.

51. Cited by Richard Feingold, "Swift in His Poems: The Range of His

Positive Rhetoric," in *The Character of Swift's Satire,* ed. Claude Rawson (Newark: University of Delaware Press, 1983), 201, fn. 20.

52. Ibid., 185.

53. Lewis Leary, *Whittier* (New York: Twayne Publishers, 1961), 169; 80.

54. Swift to Charles Wogan, July–August 1732, Williams, *Correspondence,* 4:52.

55. Williams, *Poems,* 3:968.

56. Hill, *Johnson's Lives,* 3:65.

57. Cited by Stanley Edgar Hyman, *The Armed Vision* (New York: A. A. Knopf, 1955), 65.

Chapter Five

1. Swift to Viscount Bolingbroke, Williams, *Correspondence,* 3:383.

2. Ibid., 4:40.

3. Swift to Bolingbroke and Pope, ibid., 3:329.

4. Swift to Pope, ibid., 2:366–67.

5. Davis, *Works,* 9:xxii.

6. Hawkesworth, *Works,* 1:15.

7. See Landa, *Swift and the Church of Ireland,* 191–92.

8. Ibid., 187.

9. Swift to Charles Ford, Williams, *Correspondence,* 4:505.

10. Cited by Landa, *Swift and the Church of Ireland,* 69.

11. Ibid., 192.

12. Louis Landa, *Irish Tracts and Sermons* (Oxford: Basil Blackwell, 1948), 98.

13. Swift to Rev. John Winder, Williams, *Correspondence,* 1:29.

14. Quintana, *Introduction,* 35. See pp. 33–38 for a brief but helpful discussion of what Quintana calls Swift's "Restoration Anglicanism."

15. Landa, *Irish Tracts,* 102.

16. Cited by Ehrenpreis, *Swift,* 3:75.

17. Laetitia Pilkington, *Memoirs with Anecdotes of Dr. Swift, 1748–1754* (New York: Garland Publishing, 1975); Rpt. of *The Memoirs of Mrs. Laetitia Pilkington* (Dublin and London: R. Griffiths, 1748), 52.

18. Hawkesworth, *Works,* 1:35.

19. Ehrenpreis, *Swift,* 3:77.

20. Authoritative sources for studying Swift's sermons: Louis Landa, *Swift and the Church of Ireland* and his introduction to the sermons in his *Irish Tracts and Sermons.* Ehrenpreis has an informative summary in *Swift,* 3:69–85.

21. Landa, *Irish Tracts,* 3:101.

22. Landa, *Swift and the Church of Ireland,* 91.

23. Nokes, *Jonathan Swift*, 273.

24. Pons, *Swift*, 375.

25. Nokes, *Jonathan Swift*, 101.

26. Davis, *Works*, 9:xxvii.

27. Cited by Hawkesworth, *Works*, 2:72 (footnote).

28. Davis, *Works*, 9:xxvii.

29. Cited by Katherine Hornbeak in her article on the identity of "the very young lady," in the *Huntington Library Quarterly* 7 (February 1944):184, from Mrs. Pilkington's *Memoirs*.

30. Temple Scott, *The Prose Works of Swift*, 12 vols. (London: G. Bell & Sons, 1900–8), 11:115.

31. Pons refers to this fact again and again. One of numerous examples is on page 327, for example.

32. Cited by Davis, *Works*, 12:xix–xx.

33. Price, *Rhetorical Art*, 71.

34. Williams, *Correspondence*, 2:342.

33. Oliver Ferguson, *Swift and Ireland* (Urbana: University of Illinois Press, 1962), 173.

36. Landa, *Swift and the Church of Ireland*, 195.

37. Ferguson, *Swift and Ireland*, 136, 186.

38. This quotation and those that follow (all from the *Short View*) are taken from Davis, *Works*, 12:8–11.

39. Ehrenpreis, *Swift*, 3:714.

40. Ferguson, *Swift and Ireland*, 170.

41. Davis, *Works*, 10:63.

42. Edward Rosenheim, *Swift and the Satirist's Art* (Chicago: University of Chicago Press, 1969), 47–51.

Chapter Six

1. Quintana, *Introduction*, 105.

2. These are Pope's words, cited by Quintana in *The Mind and Art of Swift*, 206.

3. Ehrenpreis, *Swift*, 3:445. Ehrenpreis gives as his authority the *Memoirs of Scriblerus*, ed. C. Kerby-Miller (New Haven: Yale University Press, 1950), 315–20.

4. Quintana, *Introduction*, 144; and for a more extended report, see William Eddy, *Gulliver's Travels: A Critical Study* (Princeton: Princeton University Press, 1923).

5. A useful summary of relevant information is in D. Nichol Smith, *The Letters of Swift to Ford* (Oxford: Oxford University Press, 1935), xxxix–xl.

6. Williams, *Correspondence*, 4:338.

7. Ibid., 102.

8. Smith, *Letters to Ford*, 158.

9. Williams, *Correspondence*, 3:179.

10. Ibid., 182.

11. See Quintana, *Mind and Art*, 303–6; and see Merrel Clubb, "The Criticism of Gulliver's 'Voyage to the Houyhnhnms,' " in *Stanford Studies in Language and Literature*, ed. Hardin Craig. (Stanford: Stanford University Press, 1941), 203–32.

12. Hill, *Johnson's Lives*, 3:38.

13. Leslie Stephen, *Swift* (London: Macmillan, 1931), 180.

14. Swift to Benjamin Motte, 28 December 1727, Williams, *Correspondence*, 3:257.

15. For the development of this idea, see John F. Ross, "Studies in the Comic," *University of California Publications in English* 8, no. 2 (1941): 175–96.

16. James Clifford, "Gulliver's Fourth Voyage: 'Hard' and 'Soft' Schools of Interpretation," in *Quick Springs of Sense: Studies of the 18th Century*, ed. Larry Champion (Athens: University of Georgia Press, 1974), 33.

17. See the footnotes to Professor Clifford's article for references to the many scholars, "hard" and "soft," who have contributed significantly to this question.

18. Clifford, "Gulliver's Fourth Voyage," 41.

19. Swift to Benjamin Motte, 28 December 1727, Williams, *Correspondence*, 3:257.

20. This interesting analysis is derived from Edward Block, "Lemuel Gulliver: Middle-class Englishman," *Modern Language Notes* 68 (November 1953):474–77.

21. Cited by Louis Landa in "Jonathan Swift," in the *Norton Critical Edition of "Gulliver's Travels*," ed. Robert Greenberg (New York: W. W. Norton & Co., 1961), 275.

22. Ehrenpreis, *The Personality of Swift*, 49.

23. Swift to Charles Wogan, July–2 August 1732), Williams, *Correspondence*, 4:52.

24. All quotations from *Gulliver's Travels* are from the Reverside edition, ed. Louis A. Landa (Boston: Houghton Mifflin, 1950).

25. Frank Brady, "Vexations and Diversions: Three Problems in *Gulliver's Travels*," *Modern Philology* 75 (1978):350.

26. See the Arthur Case edition of *Gulliver's Travels* (New York: Ronald Press, 1938), 344.

27. George Sherburn, ed., *Gulliver's Travels* (New York: Harper & Brothers, 1950), ix.

28. Hill, *Johnson's Lives*, 3:38.

29. For a contrary view, see John N. Sutherland, "A Reconsideration of Gulliver's Third Voyage," *Studies in Philology* 54 (January 1957): 45–52.

30. Kathleen Williams, "The Shadowy World of the Third Voyage" (from her *Jonathan Swift and the Age of Compromise*), included in *Norton Critical*

Edition of "Gulliver's Travels," ed. Louis Landa (Boston: Houghton Mifflin, 1960), 33.

31. Consider Kathleen Williams's above-noted essay. See, too, Marjorie Nicholson and Nora Mohler, "The Scientific Background of Swift's *Voyage to Laputa,*" *Annals of Science* 2 (July 1977):291–334, and "Swift's Flying Island" in the *Voyage to Laputa, Annals of Science* 2 (July 1977):405–30.

32. See especially the above-noted essays of Nicholson and Mohler.

33. See note 2 to this chapter.

34. Bonamy Dobrée, "Swift and Science, and the Placing of Book III," in the *Norton Critical Edition of "Gulliver's Travels,"* 330.

35. Ibid., 331.

36. Case, ed. *Gulliver's Travels,* 344.

37. Hugo Reichard, "Gulliver and the Pretender," *Papers on English Language Literature,* 1 (Autumn 1965):321, 325.

38. Brady, "Vexations and Diversions," 365.

39. Ernest Tuveson, "Swift: The Dean as Satirist," *University of Toronto Quarterly,* 22 (July 1958):368–75.

40. Landa, *Swift and the Church of Ireland,* 191–92.

41. Brady, "Vexations and Diversions," 365.

42. Wayne Booth, *The Rhetoric of Fiction* (Chicago: University of Chicago Press, 1961), 320.

43. Ross, "Studies in the Comic," 194.

Chapter Seven

1. Williams, *Poems,* 3:861 ("Lady A——S——N, Weary of the Dean").

2. Ehrenpreis, *Swift,* 3:75.

3. Davis, *Works,* 8:77 ("Some Free Thoughts upon the Present State of Affairs").

4. 11 September 1711, Williams, *Journal,* 2:357.

5. Ibid., 2:669.

6. Virginia Woolf, *Orlando: A Biography* (New York: Harcourt Brace & Co., 1928), 208–11.

7. Cited by Ehrenpreis, *Swift,* 2:1.

8. Williams, *Poems,* 3:861 ("Lady A——S——N, Weary of the Dean").

9. Quintana, *Introduction,* 27.

10. Cited from F. R. Leavis, *Determinations* (London: Faber & Faber, 1934), by John Traugott, ed., in his *Discussions of Swift,* (Boston: D. C. Heath & Co., 1962), 42.

11. Williams, *Correspondence,* 5:505.

12. Ibid., 4:529.

13. Ibid., 2:364 (1720).

Selected Bibliography

PRIMARY WORKS

Davis, Herbert et al., eds. *The Prose Works of Jonathan Swift*. 14 vols. Oxford: Oxford University Press, 1940–68.
Williams, Harold, ed. *The Correspondence of Jonathan Swift*. 5 vols. Oxford: Clarendon Press, 1963–65.
———. *The Journal to Stella*. 2 vols. Oxford: Oxford University Press, 1948.
———. *The Poems of Jonathan Swift*. 3 vols. Oxford: Oxford University Press, 1937.

SECONDARY WORKS

Bibliographies

Three essential, easy-to-find bibliographical aids are:
Landa, Louis A., and James E. Tobin, *Jonathan Swift: A List of Critical Studies Published from 1895 to 1945*. New York: Cosmopolitan Science and Art Service Co., 1945.
Stathis, James J. *A Bibliography of Swift Studies, 1945–1965*. Nashville: Vanderbilt University Press, 1967.
Veith, David. *Swift's Poetry, 1900–1980: An Annotated Bibliography*. New York: Garland Publishing Co., 1982.
These aids should be supplemented by "English Literature, 1660–1800: A Current Bibliography," which appeared annually in the *Philological Quarterly* until 1970 and has since been succeeded by *The Eighteenth Century: A Current Bibliography*.

Books

Barnett, Louise K. *Swift's Poetic Works*. Newark: University of Delaware Press; London and Toronto: Associated University Presses, 1981. An attractive study, but thought by some to be uneven.
Brown, Norman. *Life Against Death: The Psychoanalytical Meaning of History*. Middletown, Conn.: Wesleyan University Press, 1959. This book contains the well-known chapter on what is called "The Excremental Vision" of Jonathan Swift.
Bullitt, John M. *Jonathan Swift and the Anatomy of Satire*. Cambridge: Harvard

University Press, 1953. Attempts to define three types of satiric technique used by Swift.

Craik, Henry. *The Life of Swift.* 2 vols. London: Murray, 1882. Still one of the best full-length biographies of Swift.

Delaney, Patrick. *Observations upon Lord Orrery's Remarks.* London: 1754. The best of the books written by a person who knew Swift.

Downie, J. A. *Jonathan Swift: Political Writer.* London: Routledge & Kegan Paul, 1984. A useful and authoritative study focusing on Swift's political writings.

Eddy, William A. *"Gulliver's Travels." A Critical Study.* Princeton: Princeton University Press, 1923. The first great book-length study of the sources of *Gulliver's Travels,* it must be supplemented today by more modern investigations.

Ehrenpreis, Irvin. *The Personality of Swift.* London: Methuen & Co., 1958. Significant biographical material. Opinions somewhat changed in the author's later works.

————. *Swift: The Man, His Works, and The Age.* 3 vols. London: Methuen & Co., 1962 (vol. 1), 1967 (vol. 2); Cambridge: Harvard University Press, 1983 (vol. 3). These three volumes are the impressive results of more than two decades of work by one of the more formidable and expert researchers of our times. Some readers find the penchant for psychological speculation not entirely to their taste. The three volumes must nonetheless be regarded as an indispensable tool for any serious student of Swift.

Elias, A. C., Jr. *Swift at Moor Park: Problems in Biography and Criticism.* Philadelphia: University of Pennsylvania Press, 1982. A provocative but carefully wrought contribution to Swift studies.

England, A. B. *Energy and Order in the Poetry of Swift.* Lewisburg: Bucknell University Press; London and Toronto: Associated University Presses, 1980. One of the best of the recent books on Swift's poetry. Poems are selected and analyzed to illustrate stylistic tendencies ("Energy" and "Order") in Swift's poetry.

Ewald, William Bragg, Jr. *The Masks of Jonathan Swift.* New Haven: Yale University Press, 1954. An outstanding study of Swift's use of personae.

Fischer, John Irwin. *On Swift's Poetry.* Gainesville: University Presses of Florida, 1978. A distinguished contribution to the growing interest in Swift's poetry. Learned, careful, detailed analysis of selected poems.

Ferguson, Oliver. *Swift and Ireland.* Urbana: University of Illinois Press, 1962. With Landa's books, this has become a standard source of information about Swift's life in Ireland.

Greenacre, Phyllis. *Swift and Carroll, a Psychoanalytic Study of Two Lives.* New York: International Universities Press, 1955. The psychoanalysts find Swift an interesting case-study.

Guthkelch, A. C., ed. *The Battle of the Books; with Selections from the Literature of the Phalaris Controversy.* London: Chatto, 1908. An essential source for the study of the *Battle*.

———, and D. Nichol Smith, eds. *A Tale of a Tub, The Battle of the Books, and The Mechanical Operation of the Spirit.* Oxford: Oxford University Press, 1920. Still a reliable and extremely useful book.

Harth, Philip. *Swift and Anglican Rationalism: The Religious Background of "A Tale of a Tub."* Chicago: University of Chicago Press, 1961. A careful and judicious investigation, particularly interesting in its references to the two voices—Swift's and the hack's—in the *Tale of a Tub*.

Jaffe, Nora Crow. *The Poet Swift.* Hanover, N.H.: University Press of New England, 1977. The generalization about Swift's poetry might disturb some readers. Excellent close readings of the poems, however.

Johnson, Maurice. *The Sin of Wit: Jonathan Swift as a Poet.* Syracuse: Syracuse University Press, 1950. For a whole generation of readers in the 1950s and 1960s this was about the best critical book on Swift's poetry available.

Landa, Louis, ed. *Jonathan Swift: Irish Tracts and Sermons.* Oxford: Basil Blackwell, 1948.

———. *Swift and the Church of Ireland.* Oxford: Clarendon Press, 1954. Landa's two books are valuable statements about Swift's life and his writings in Ireland.

McHugh, Roger, and Philip Edwards, eds. *Jonathan Swift, 1667–1967, Dublin Tercentenary Tribute.* Dublin: Dolman Press, 1967. A distinguished collection of essays by eleven well-known contemporary scholars.

Nokes, David. *Jonathan Swift, a Hypocrite Reversed: A Critical Biography.* Oxford: Oxford University Press, 1985. An excellent and up-to-date biography for the general reader.

Paulson, Ronald. *Theme and Structure in Swift's "Tale of a Tub."* New Haven: Yale University Press, 1960. An influential examination of Swift's great book.

Pilkington, Lætitia. *Memoirs with Anecdotes of Dean Swift, 1748–1754.* New York: Garland Publishing, 1975. Reprint of *The Memoirs of Mrs. Lætitia Pilkington* (Dublin and London: R. Griffiths, 1748). Lively if not always reliable recollections of a person who knew Swift. Monck Berkeley called her a "lying gossip."

Pons, Émile. *Swift; les années de jeunesse et le "Conte du Tonneau."* Strasbourg: Publications de la faculté des lettres de Strasbourg, 1925. A classic of Swift criticism, this great book remains a germinal text.

Price, Martin. *Swift's Rhetorical Art.* New Haven: Yale University Press, 1953. An analysis of Swift's satiric technique.

Quintana, Ricardo. *Swift: An Introduction.* London: Oxford University Press, 1955.

————. *The Mind and Art of Jonathan Swift*. London: Oxford University Press, 1936 (reprinted with additional bibliographical material, 1953). These are two great books by an eminent Swift scholar.

Rawson, Claude, ed. *The Character of Swift's Satire*. Newark: University of Delaware Press, 1983. A fine collection of essays, including among others John Traugott's incisive "A Tale of a Tub" and Richard Feingold's helpful "Swift in His Poems: The Range of His Positive Rhetoric."

Schakel, Peter J. *The Poetry of Jonathan Swift: Allusion and the Development of a Poetic Style*. Madison: University of Wisconsin Press, 1978. Deservedly highly regarded criticism that bears witness to the increased interest in Swift's poetry.

Sheridan, Thomas. *The Life of the Rev. Dr. Jonathan Swift, Dean of St. Patrick's, Dublin*. London, 1784. Reprinted, New York: Garland Publishing, 1974. Richly anecdotal and full of charm, but as a biography frequently unreliable.

Starkman, Miriam. *Swift's Satire on Learning in "A Tale of a Tub."* Princeton: Princeton University Press, 1950. A scholarly discussion of the satire in *A Tale of a Tub*.

Vieth, David, ed. *Essential Articles for the Study of Jonathan Swift's Poetry*. Hamden, Conn.: Archon Books, 1984. A very welcome and extremely valuable collection of essays including, among others, those by Roger Savage ("Swift's Fallen City: 'A Description of the Morning' "), Brendan O Hehir ("Meaning of Swift's 'Description of A City Shower' "), John M. Aden ("Corinna and the Sterner Muse of Swift"), and Richard Rodino ("Blasphemy or Blessing? Swift's 'Scatological Poems' ").

Watkins, W. B. C. *Perilous Balance: The Tragic Genius of Swift, Johnson, and Sterne*. Princeton: Princeton University Press, 1939. See especially chapter 1 (on Swift) and chapter 2 (on Swift and Johnson).

Williams, Kathleen. *Swift and the Age of Compromise*. Lawrence: University of Kansas Press, 1958. A close study of Swift's understanding and use of the concept of Reason.

Articles

Adams, R. M. "Jonathan Swift, Thomas Swift, and the Authorship of *A Tale of A Tub*." *Modern Philology* 64 (1967):198–202. Adams argues for a dual-authorship by these cousins.

Block, Edward. "Gulliver: Middle-Class Englishman." *Modern Language Notes* 68 (November 1953):474–77. An intriguing reading of the opening lines of *Gulliver's Travels*.

Brady, Frank. "Vexations and Diversions: Three Problems in *Gulliver's Travels*." *Modern Philology* 75 (1978):346–67. A careful, scholarly, readable, and persuasive essay.

Brown, James. "Swift as Moralist." *Philological Quarterly* 33 (1954):368–87. A valuable discussion of an always much-mooted question.

Clifford, James. "Gulliver's Fourth Voyage: 'Hard' and 'Soft' Schools of Interpretation." In *Quick Springs of Sense: Studies in the 18th Century,* edited by Larry Champion, 33–49. Athens: University of Georgia Press, 1974.

Clubb, Mérrel D. "The Criticism of Gulliver's 'Voyage to the Houyhnhnms,' 1726–1914." In *Stanford Studies in Language and Literature,* edited by Hardin Craig, 203–32. Stanford: Stanford University Press, 1941. A fascinating report of the changing critical response to book 4 of *Gulliver's Travels.*

Elliott, Robert C. "Gulliver as Literary Artist." *Journal of English Literary History* 19 (1952):49–63. Gulliver is seen as a talented writer, objective, and capable even of irony.

Johnson, Maurice. "A Literary Chestnut: Dryden's 'Cousin Swift.' " *PMLA* 66 (1952): 1024–34. Johnson gives the facts that disprove this oft-heard tale.

Landa, Louis A. "Swift's Economic Views of Mercantilism." *Journal of English Literary History* 10 (December 1943):310–33. Information here is particularly important to a reading of *The Drapier Letters* and *A Modest Proposal.*

Nicholson, Marjorie and Nora Mohler. "The Scientific Background of Swift's *Voyage to Laputa.*" *Annals of Science* 2 (July 1937):291–334.

————. "Swift's Flying Island in the *Voyage to Laputa.*" *Annals of Science* 2 (July 1937):405–30. These two articles revised conventional opinions about book 3 of *Gulliver's Travels.*

Ross, John F. "The Final Comedy of Lemuel Gulliver." In *Studies in the Comic (University of California Publications in English,* Berkeley) 8, no. 2 (1941). Creative criticism that helped pioneer a breakthrough in the reading of book 4 of *Gulliver's Travels.*

Webster, C. M. "Swift's *Tale of a Tub* Compared with Earlier Satires of the Puritans." *PMLA* 47 (1933):171–78.

————. "Swift and Some Earlier Satirists of Puritan Enthusiasm." *PMLA* 48 (1933):1141–53. These two pioneer studies are still relied upon in any discussion of Swift's comments about the Puritans.

Index